ALIENATED

JEFF DUNN

21ST CENTURY CHRISTIAN

Alienated

ISBN: 978-0-89098-947-0

©2024 by 21st Century Christian, Inc
Nashville, TN 37215
All rights reserved.

All rights reserved. No part of this publication may be reproduced, stored in a retrieval system, or transmitted in any form or by any means—electronic, mechanical, photocopy, recording, digital, or otherwise—without the written
permission of the publisher.

Unless otherwise noted, Scripture quotations are from the ESV® Bible (The Holy Bible, English Standard Version®), © 2001 by Crossway, a publishing ministry of Good News Publishers. Used by permission. All rights reserved.

Scripture quotations marked (NASB®) are from the New American Standard Bible®, Copyright © 1960, 1971, 1977, 1995, 2020 by The Lockman Foundation. Used by permission. All rights reserved. lockman.org

Scripture quotations marked (NASB® 1995) are from the New American Standard Bible®, Copyright © 1960, 1971, 1977, 1995 by The Lockman Foundation. Used by permission. All rights reserved. lockman.org

Scripture quotations marked (KJV) are from the King James Version. Public domain.

Scripture quotations marked (NIV) are from the Holy Bible, New International Version®, NIV®. Copyright © 1973, 1978, 1984, 2011 by Biblica, Inc.™ Used by permission of Zondervan. All rights reserved worldwide. www.zondervan.com The "NIV" and "New International Version" are trademarks registered in the United States Patent and Trademark Office by Biblica, Inc.™

Scripture quotations marked (CSB) are from the Christian Standard Bible®, Copyright © 2017 by Holman Bible Publishers. Used by permission. Christian Standard Bible® and CSB® are federally registered trademarks of Holman Bible Publishers.

Cover design by Jared Kendall

Table of Contents

1. Alien Identity 5
2. The Mystery of Salvation 19
3. Girded for Grace 27
4. Building Blocks 39
5. Alien Behavior 53
6. Alien Blood 65
7. Alien Membership 75
8. Alien Trials 87
9. Alien Leaders 103
10. Alien Burdens 111
11. Lions, Suffering, and Glory (Oh, My!) 127
12. Living in an Alien Nation 143

CHAPTER ONE

Alien Identity

"I've always felt like an alien trapped in a human form . . . and I'm still unsure if Earth is a penance or a reward."
— Douglas Coupland

I've never really had a nickname. I guess technically, Jeff, is a nickname because my actual name is Jeffrey. But the truth is, I don't answer to Jeffrey. The only people who call me that are my mom, my father-in-law, and Hilary — when she's really mad at me.

A while back, I asked my social media followers to share their nicknames. It was a lot of fun because I got to see a different side of many people in my life. In the responses to that post and the subsequent replies, we got some great ones. Names like Tyke, Blueberry, Olive, a couple of those who go by Grace, Si, Sal-Gal, Cotton, M&MSpootnik, Gram, and Nana.

I used to give a lot of nicknames. I still do. My girls listed about 10 a piece one night at dinner when I asked them what I called them.

ALIENATED

A few years ago, I remember one of my former youth group kids was introducing me to her new husband. I called her "Pud." When she was little, I nicknamed her "Puddin," which was shortened to "Pud." Now she's 25 years old. I hug her and ask, "Hey, Pud, how are you?" Her husband laughs and questions, "Pud?" She shoots him a sheepish grin and says, "This man right here is the ONLY person in the world who can call me that and not get hurt. Do you understand?!"

Nicknames help establish our identity. We either conform to the name or somehow try to live it down. Many times, we simply grow out of it or change so that it no longer applies. Sometimes, nicknames are part of who we are, but other times they become labels that keep us from being who we wish to be.

Nicknames originate from different points of view:

- a quality, for example "Sugar" (sweet);
- an incident, as was the case with "Wheaties";
- a verbal analogy, in Japan a woman named Marlene was transposed to "Maagarin," (margarine in Japanese);
- physical attributes, "Slim" (tall and thin);
- animal or other associations, Jackie Amos became "Mosquito," a woman born in the summer was "June Bug," which later became simply, "Bug";
- a folk or popular character, Donald became "Duck" for Donald Duck;
- rhyming words, Harris became "Paris";
- adding a suffix or prefix, as "ie" became Jackie;
- an abbreviation of the name, Daniel became "Dan," and on and on it goes. Nicknames are as diverse as the cultures from which they might originate.

A study conducted by Albert Mehrabian and Marlena Pierce in 1993 found that "given names were ranked high on the attributes of success and morality and thought more suitable (than nicknames) for business and professional settings. In turn, nicknames were ranked high on the attributes of cheerfulness and popularity." The choice of names people go by is not fixed. A person may use his given name in business settings and his nickname in social settings.

Research confirms what we all anecdotally know to be true; nicknames are associated with stronger relationships. We award nicknames to the people (and pets) in our lives with whom we feel a special bond.

Suzanne Degges-White, a counselor and professor at Northern Illinois University, has extensively studied friendships and familial relationships. She says "couplespeak"— inside jokes and nicknames used by people in love — develop over time in happy partnerships.

"As couples get closer and their relationships build, the use of personal idioms and inside jokes increases," Degges-White writes in Psychology Today. "In fact, research shows that personal idiom usage is a sign of relationship solidarity."

Peter is a guy who has his name changed. However, it isn't really that simple.

Jesus does not give nicknames, but He does give new names. In fact, the same Peter who's writing this letter that we'll be studying has an encounter with Jesus. Jesus gives him a new name, not a nickname, but a new name.

The story in question is recounted in John 1:35–42. Peter's brother, Andrew, has started following Jesus. One of the two who heard John speak and followed Jesus was Andrew, Simon Peter's brother. He first found his own brother Simon and said to him, "We have found the Messiah" (which means Christ). It's the Anointed One. It's the waited for one of the nation of Israel. The culmination of Israel's hope. Andrew says to his brother, "We have found the Messiah!" He brought him to Jesus. Jesus looked at him and said, "You are Simon the son of John. You shall be called Cephas" (ESV). In the Greek, it's Petros or Peter.

Only Jesus, upon just meeting someone, could say, "That's a great name. I know you've lived with it since birth, but it doesn't quite do justice to where I'm going to take you. You are no longer Simon; now you're Peter." Because Peter used that name the rest of his life, which means when Jesus changes your name, your only response is OK. What is Jesus doing? He's saying to Peter, "Who you are now cannot encapsulate, cannot contain, all that I'm going to do in your life. So Peter, I'm not just going to give you a nickname, I'm not just going to amend you a little bit . . . I'm not just going to shave off some of the rough edges. Peter, what I'm going to do is make you completely new. I'm going to make you completely different, so much so that even your name will change. Peter, you're going to be born again. You're going to be born anew. You're going to be born afresh. Life from this moment forward, Peter, because of what I'm doing, is going to be different."

Just like He does with Abram or with Jacob, God has the power to rewrite your story. And when He does, He gives you a new name that is known to Him because He sees the totality of who you are and who you will become in Him. This is not just a nickname; this is a new identity.

According to psychologists, there are three major perspectives in explaining the identity and how we become who we are. The first one is **social identity theory** in which the founders see group membership as the driving force for identity formation. The next theory is **identity theory**, in which roles that are assigned to individuals are deemed as the major source for energy to identity formation. The last theory, **personal identity theory**, talks about the importance of personal values in explaining the identity and identity formation process.

Peter, however, encounters a fourth identity shaper — Jesus. When we meet Jesus and have a true encounter with Him, our identity is forever changed. Our individuality is no longer shaped by group membership, individual roles, or personal values. Instead, our identity becomes inexorably connected with the overwhelming presence of Jesus Christ.

That's what happens to Peter.

This same Peter is the impetuous one. The hothead. The mouth. He's the guy who blurts out what everyone else is thinking even if it's totally inappropriate. He's the guy who is the first one there, charging in blindly. Of course, he's also the first one to run away. He's the guy who is big talk until the chips are down, then he's nowhere to be found. When the authorities come to arrest Jesus, guess who is wielding a sword? Peter!

He's the guy who jumps out of the boat. When Jesus is walking on the water, Peter is the one who cries, "Lord, tell me to come to you, and I will!" A lot of times I hear preachers focus in on Peter's lack of faith, but remember, there were at least 11 other guys in that boat, and NONE of them even entertained the idea of getting out of it! Peter is so overwhelmed with faith and trust in Jesus that he DOES walk on the water. He gets out there. Of course, he immediately realizes the incredible impossibility of what he's doing and sinks.

He's the guy that God more or less tells to pipe down and be quiet. Think about that. (There will be some readers who are uncomfortable by my describing the situation this way, but it's totally what God tells Peter.) Let me set the scene. Jesus takes Peter, James, and John up the mount. They're hanging out, having a good time, and BOOM — Moses and Elijah show up! And the disciples lose it! I mean, they totally geek out!

I remember when we took our youngest daughter to Disney World for the first time. She was about three years old, and she was so overwhelmed! She could hardly speak! She was not standing next to characters or actors in costume; she WAS ACTUALLY MEETING REAL PRINCESSES!!! And it freaked her out!

Like my daughter, the apostles freak out here on the mount of Transfiguration. Why wouldn't they freak out? Here were Moses and

ALIENATED

Elijah standing next to them! This is beyond belief! And Peter starts running off at the mouth.

"It's good to be here! This is holy ground! We'll build some altars, some temples right here. It'll be great! We'll have one over there, and we'll build another one over there . . ."

And God says, "THIS ONE IS MY SON! LISTEN TO HIM!"

> ⁵Then a voice came out of the cloud, saying, "This is My Son, My Chosen One; listen to Him!" (Luke 9:35, NASB1995).

But that isn't the only time he gets called down by God. If it isn't enough that God tells you to shut your mouth, later the Son of God calls him SATAN!

Peter took Him aside and began to rebuke Him, saying, "'God forbid it, Lord! This shall never happen to You!' But He turned and said to Peter, 'Get behind Me, Satan! You are a stumbling block to Me; for you are not setting your mind on God's purposes, but men's'" (Matthew 16:23, NASB).

Here's what Peter is basically saying to Jesus: Now Jesus, You don't need to talk like that. All that fatalistic thinking is gonna drag You down! You need to name it and claim it! You need to be more positive. If You believe it, You can receive it!" Jesus stops Peter and commands, "Stop it, Satan!"

He is sifted. His faith is shaken to its very core. Later on, when he's going to talk about the testing of one's faith in First Peter, you can be assured he understands what he is talking about because he's been there. Peter is told at the last supper that Satan is coming for him. I'm not sure I can think of anything scarier.

> "Simon, Simon, behold, Satan has demanded permission to sift you men like wheat; but I have prayed for you, that your faith will not fail; and you, when you have turned back, strengthen your brothers" (Luke 22:31–32).

Turn to when Jesus is being tried before the crucifixion. That's when Peter crashes and burns. He fails. He denies even knowing Jesus — just like Jesus said he would! Peter claims never to have heard of Him. Here's one of the most heart-wrenching pictures in Scripture:

> "But Peter said, 'Man, I do not know what you are talking about.' And immediately, while he was still speaking, a rooster crowed. And then the Lord turned and looked at Peter. And Peter remembered the word of the Lord, how He had said to him, 'Before a rooster crows today, you will deny Me three times.' And he went out and wept bitterly" (Luke 22:60–62).

Can you imagine the grief that pierces Peter's heart? Can you imagine the guilt? And at the risk of going off on a tangent, how amazing is it that at His trial, as the ruler with the power to crucify is questioning him, Jesus' attention was on the faith of one weak believer. He isn't looking at Pilate, He isn'tt defending Himself or even seeming interested in the trial. But at the exact moment, He turns and looks at Peter. Because He is more worried about Peter's fate than His own.

If the story ended there, it would be a tragedy or a cautionary tale. We might read the words of Peter to find out what NOT to do. We would learn how his failure was something that shaped his life in such a way that he was able to grow and prosper from it. But that isn't the end of the story.

Less than two months from the time of that denial and less than two months after those bitter tears, that same Peter would stand in front of all Jerusalem. In front of the assembled masses gathered from all nations and walks of life, in front of high priests and temple guards, in front of Pharisees and Teachers of the Law, and that same Peter admonishes them, "GOD CAME DOWN AND DWELT AMONG US. YOU KILLED HIM. BUT HE'S RISEN AGAIN!"

Later, in Acts 3, we'll read about Peter and John healing a man at the Temple. This man is there just outside the presence of God. He is excluded and pushed aside because of his imperfections. Peter and John do not merely give him physical healing; they grant him access to the presence of God. Jesus changes everything, and His resurrection paves the way for those previously unclean to be allowed access directly to God.

And after the man is healed, Peter addresses the gathered crowd in verse 12, chiding them, "Why are you amazed?" That's hilarious! You want to say, *Hey, Peter, two months ago you would have been surprised.* But Peter is changed. He is not the same man he was two months ago. Shaky Simon has been replaced by "The Rock," and he asks, "Why you are you amazed?"

Peter begins preaching and says in verse 17, "I know that you acted in ignorance, just as did your rulers" (NASB). Again, I find that amusing. He's in the temple. In the temple, they have men called temple guards. Armed guards. Armed guards who served those same leaders that Peter just called ignorant. Those same leaders that Peter just accused of killing the Messiah. But do we ever see the same cowardly, cowering Peter that we saw before? No! Instead, we see a brave champion of the church!

So what changed? What changed to turn Peter from zero to hero? What changed inside him that made him so fearless and courageous? Well, it's the one thing that should make all of us fearless and courageous: the resurrection of Jesus.

The Peter we see after the death of Jesus is remorseful. He is full of grief and pain. He is beating himself up for his failure. He is lost.

The disciples go out fishing in John 21 because that's what many of us do when we experience failure; we return to our roots. We retreat. We hide in the comfortable, the predictable, that which we understand and are able to control. So, Peter joins his buddies when they go fishing.

Alien Identity

Jesus appears on the shore and calls out "Children, do you have any fish?" (John 21:5). He tells them to cast their net on the other side, and immediately, it is so full that all of them together cannot haul it in. John whispers to Peter in astonishment, "It is the Lord!"

Peter can't wait. He jumps out of the boat and swims to shore. It's roughly a 100-yard swim fully clothed. He is so full of guilt and pain and anxiety that he is unable to control himself. Jesus invites them to breakfast. Peter is so jacked up, so full of nervous energy that he goes and drags that net full of fish (remember, the net that was so heavy they couldn't lift it) onto the shore.

Why is he so nervous?

You must remember; Peter is a Jew who has heard of God all his life. He has heard how God struck Uzzah down for touching the Ark. He has heard how Sodom and Gomorrah were consumed in fire for being inhospitable. He has read the passages about betrayal in synagogue from his youth.

> A false witness will not go unpunished, and he who breathes out lies will not escape (Proverbs 19:5).
>
> No one who practices deceit shall dwell in my house; no one who utters lies shall continue before my eyes (Psalm 101:7).

He has sung these psalms like Psalm 55 in church:

> For it is not an enemy who taunts me —
>   then I could bear it;
> it is not an adversary who deals insolently with me —
>   then I could hide from him.
> But it is you, a man, my equal, my
>   companion, my familiar friend.
> We used to take sweet counsel together; within
>   God's house we walked in the throng.
> Let death steal over them;

> let them go down to Sheol alive;
> for evil is in their dwelling place and in their heart (12–15).

So now you are meeting the risen Lord, the promised Messiah, the Chosen One who will lead the renewal of Israel, the One who has defeated the grave; you are about to meet Him whose power is unlike anything ever seen by man! But this is also the One who you have betrayed. What do you think he thinks is going to happen?

But what happens is, Jesus tells him, "Feed my Sheep." Jesus says to him, "Follow Me." Jesus says to him, Peter this is about new life. This is about new hope.

You see God is not in the business of making bad people good. God is not in the business of making good people better. That's good advice, but it isn't good news.

If you're a follower of Jesus, He has said the exact same thing to you! Jesus didn't die to make you more moral. Jesus didn't die to make you a better person. He died to make you a new creation. He says to you as a follower of His today, *I'm making you new. I long for you to be born again.*

Look at the way that Peter says it in his letter to the churches throughout Turkey. He says In 1 Peter 1:3: "Blessed be the God and Father of our Lord Jesus Christ! According to his great mercy, he has caused us to be born again."

In our culture, the terminology "born again" has a fair amount of baggage, does it not? When we hear that term, we think of a certain kind of people. There is a certain brand of believers that refer to themselves as "born-again Christians." They're the sort of crazy, fanatic Christians, right? Stay away! Don't go near them. Keep them at a distance. Then there are the "normal" Christians who just look a lot like everyone else.

Here's the thing about that: It isn't biblical. Did you know there's no such thing as a "non born-again Christian" in the Scriptures?

Born-again *Christian* is redundantly redundant! You are a Christian if you are born again, and if you're born again, you are a Christian. It's saying the same thing. You've never laid eyes on a follower of Jesus who isn't born again.

This is beautiful, breathtaking news for you and me. Here's the point: God is interested NOT in making bad people good. God is interested in making dead people alive.

I grew up with a gospel that sounded a lot more like good advice than good news. Anybody else? The gospel I heard was . . . "Here's the way you're supposed to look. Here's what you're supposed to do. Here's the way you're supposed to act." This is the true gospel.

The gospel — the good news — is a declaration, an announcement about what Jesus has done and who Jesus is . . . simply that! It's an announcement. It's news, not "good advice."

Like God, Jesus is interested NOT in making bad people good; He's interested in making dead people alive!

That resurrection, that new life, that new hope changes Peter. And Simon, son of John, is now the Rock, Cephas, Peter.

Peter writes to those who are scattered and enduring various persecutions throughout the region of Turkey. He calls them aliens.

Three times in the first section of this letter he will refer to them as aliens. (See 1:1, 1:17, 2:11, NASB1995).

Three times he will tell them that this world is not their home. This applies to you, too. Your kingdom is not here. Your world is not this world. Your country is not this country. Your constitution is not this constitution. So, it really doesn't matter who this country chooses to put on its money. You don't belong here. You don't live here. You are not of this world. You are an alien.

We are aliens. The language and values and customs and expectations of this world feel foreign to us. Something really radical has happened to us. Peter says in 1:3, "God . . . has caused us to be born again to a living hope" — for another world, another, greater kind of existence. Paul put it this way:

> "For you have died and your life is hidden with Christ in God. When Christ, who is our life, is revealed, then you also will be revealed with Him in glory" (Colossians 3:3–4, NASB).

Jesus called us to live like aliens — to fix our minds on radically different priorities than the nations.

Living as aliens in the world is the only pathway to heaven. If you choose to be at home in the world and love the things of the world, you will perish with the world. John said, "The world is passing away along with its desires, but whoever does the will of God abides forever" (1 John 2:17).

So how can we do that? How do we live as aliens in a foreign land?

That's the purpose of First Peter. Peter is writing to tell us that struggling and failing is okay. He's done it. He's made it through. It tested his faith and solidified it; purified it; burned away the impurities and strengthened it.

How do we maintain our alien mindset and focus? How do we stay connected to a new birth and a new hope when all around us is hopelessness and death?

Skip with me to 1 Peter 4:7–10.

> The end of all things is at hand; therefore be self-controlled and sober-minded for the sake of your prayers. Above all, keep loving one another earnestly, since love covers a multitude of sins. Show hospitality to one another without grumbling. As each has received a gift, use it to serve one another, as good stewards of God's varied grace:

Sober-minded prayers, love for one another, hospitality, and service.

Alien Identity

This book is about joining in that journey. Stepping out in faith, like Peter, away from our comfort zones and the familiarity of what we have always known and living like aliens. Living in a world where we don't belong in a way that doesn't match up with the values and focus of the world around us. Can we do that?

We don't just want to be good citizens. We don't want to merely be good people. We want to be new creatures. New creations. Totally made over in the image of the One we follow.

So, if you have a gift of hospitality, you open your home, your life, your heart to the people God places in your life.

If you have a gift to teach, you find ways to share your knowledge, your wisdom, your experience, all the things that God has placed on your heart. You find a way to share that with others who may desperately need that in their lives.

When we share in this new hope, in this new birth, in this new life together as we combine our hearts to seek the inheritance God is preserving us for in Christ Jesus, we move from being citizens of a lost and dying world to aliens.

We also find a new name in Jesus Christ. No longer am I merely Jeff, instead I am renamed. I am made new. I am no longer Jeff, instead I am Christian — one who has been called out and branded — renamed by my Lord and renewed into a totally different creature.

I pray this study leads us into an alien existence. I pray that it remakes our hearts with a longing for home and a commitment to live as strangers in this world.

We walk together as those who are alienated, as a group of refugees living in a foreign land. We hold together in the hope of eternity and lift one another up in the fullness of salvation.

Remember, God is not in the business of making bad people good or good people better; He is at work making dead people alive.

Let's seek that new life together.

ALIENATED

Discussion Questions

1. What are some nicknames that you have had?
2. Why do you think the Bible shows us stories like Peter's without editing out the failures? Why not "clean it up" and make Peter into a hero instead of showing us the ways he messed up or struggled?
3. What do you think of when you hear the phrase "born again?" How is the usage of that phrase in modern America different or similar to the way Peter is using it?
4. When you think of being an alien, what does that entail in your mind?
5. How can you and I be aliens in the world today?
6. How has the church missed the teaching that God wants to make dead people alive? How have we taught that God just wants to make good people better?
7. How does a new name, a new birth, a new identity change the way we interact with the world around us?

CHAPTER TWO

The Mystery of Salvation

"Perhaps we need some outside, universal threat to make us recognize this common bond. I occasionally think how quickly our differences worldwide would vanish if we were facing an alien threat from outside this world."
— **Ronald Reagan**

How do you think inspiration worked? Most of us, as Christians believe that the Bible is the inspired word of God. So how did that inspiration work? I mean, we don't have any direct writings that told us how it worked, so let's imagine for a minute. How do you think it worked?

Pretend you're Isaiah or maybe Micah, how do you think it worked?

Some believe it was direct dictation. That means God said exactly what He wanted written. In eighth grade, Mr. Eberlan made us keep a homework journal every day. He would begin class every day with dictation of our assignments: "In spelling, comma, write the following words *semicolon* . . . and on and on." A lot of people believe that is how God's inspiration worked.

Others see it as a scene in the movies in which a person is overcome and begins spewing things with no understanding of what they are doing. So, God just starts writing through your hands, and before you know it, you've completed a prophesy.

Do you think the prophet ever looked at what he wrote and thought, *Wow, I wonder what that means?* Yeah, I think so too!

So did Peter. Read 1 Peter 1:10–12:

> Concerning this salvation, the prophets who prophesied about the grace that was to be yours searched and inquired carefully, inquiring what person or time the Spirit of Christ in them was indicating when he predicted the sufferings of Christ and the subsequent glories. It was revealed to them that they were serving not themselves but you, in the things that have now been announced to you through those who preached the good news to you by the Holy Spirit sent from heaven, things into which angels long to look.

Jesus said to his disciples once, "Blessed are your eyes, because they see; and your ears, because they hear. For truly I say to you, that many prophets and righteous people longed to see what you see, and did not see it; and to hear what you hear, and did not hear it" (Matthew 13:16–17, NASB).

So the main point of this paragraph is that we should be amazed at the greatness of our salvation and that this greatness is demonstrated by the fact that prophets of God and angels of heaven long to look into it.

Salvation means being saved. So why do we need to be saved? This is the question of the age. . . . Children who have grown up in churches where their parents are nominally committed and apathetic do not feel a need to be saved. Non-Christians living in a culture of acceptance and tolerance, where everything is okay, and each person has their own "truth" do not feel a need to be saved.

There are even people who profess to be believers and Christians who feel no need to ask for forgiveness, no need to be saved.

So, from what do we need to be saved?

In 1 Peter 2:24 Peter says, "[Christ] Himself bore our sins in His body on the cross, so that we might die to sin and live to righteousness; for by His wounds you were healed." Christ bore our sins because we need to be saved from our sins. They are like a terminal disease that will kill us forever. Christ's wounds can heal that disease.

In 1 Peter 3:18 we read, "Christ also died for sins once for all, the just for the unjust, so that He might bring us to God" (NASB1995). Christ died for our sins because we need to be saved from our sins. They separate us from God. So Christ died for our sins to bring us home to God.

In 1 Peter 4:17 he teaches us, "It is time for judgment to begin with the household of God; and if it begins with us first, what will be the outcome for those who do not obey the gospel of God?"

We need to be saved from God's judgment. Sin is not just a terminal disease that needs healing. It is also terminal guilt that deserves judgment. The gospel is the good news that Christ bears the judgment of all who trust Him.

In 1 Peter 5:8, Peter says, "Your adversary, the devil, prowls about like a roaring lion, seeking someone to devour." In other words, you need to be saved from the devil who is a liar and a murderer and is trying to destroy as many human beings as he can. He is a lion, which means he is far more powerful than you or I, so we need salvation from him. The Bible says that the Son of God came into the world to destroy the works of the devil (1 John 3:8). Peter says resist him in our faith.

Again, from what do we need to be saved? Peter's answer is — We need to be saved from the disease and guilt of sin, from the judgment of God, and from the destruction of the devil. The question you need to answer now is: Are you in danger? Is Peter telling the truth? Do you need to be saved?

ALIENATED

But it's not just about what we need to be saved *from*, it's about what we need to be saved *for*...

In 1 Peter 2:25 Peter says, "You were continually straying like sheep, but now you have returned to the Shepherd and Guardian of your souls." Salvation means being brought home to a loving Shepherd who will lead us in green pastures and by still waters.

Then in 1 Peter 5:4 he says, "When [this] Chief Shepherd appears [at his second coming], you will receive the unfading crown of glory." This is the "unfading" inheritance of verse 4. That means, we are saved for an inheritance of glory. No more shame, but honor. No more disgrace or humiliation but the revelation of the glory of the children of God.

First Peter 5:10 says that God called us to this: "The God of all grace... has called you to His eternal glory in Christ." We are saved to share in the glory of Christ. The result of this will, of course, be everlasting joy: "To the degree that you share the sufferings of Christ, keep on rejoicing; so that also at the revelation of His glory, you may rejoice with exultation (1 Peter 4:13, NASB1995).

That's what we are saved *for*: a relationship with Christ the Shepherd of our soul, a participation in the eternal glory of God, and a joy as eternal as the glory.

The word of God — not the word of the newspaper editorialists, not the word of the television, not the word of public schools, not the word of state universities — but the word of the apostle Peter, speaking on behalf of Jesus

Christ the Son of God, who expresses the very mind of God is this: We need to be saved.

Saved from sin and Satan and judgment. And saved for inexpressible joy with the Shepherd of our souls in light of the glory of God for ever and ever.

So in verse 10 when Peter says, "As to this salvation..." we now have some idea of what he's talking about. His aim in verses 10–12

The Mystery of Salvation

is to intensify our gratitude and fill us with joy and worship for the infinite value of this great salvation.

He does this by telling us five amazing things about our salvation — things that we may have never thought of before. I will briefly mention them and pray they will stick in your heart and bear the fruit of faith and thanksgiving.

Christ Predicted It

Peter points out the amazing fact that Christ Himself—the Spirit of Christ — hundreds of years before His own death and resurrection was predicting His own death and resurrection. Look at the middle of 1 Peter 1:11: "The Spirit of Christ within [the prophets] . . . predicted the sufferings of Christ and the glories to follow."

Christ predicted the sufferings of Christ.

Yes, you read that correctly, which means that Christ, the Son of God in heaven, contemplated His suffering and death for us for centuries. Indeed, as far back as the plan of salvation reaches in the mind of God, so far back has Christ been willing and ready to give Himself for our sins. You were not loved for just a bloody moment of sacrifice in history. You have been loved for endless ages in the eternal plan of the Father and the Son to save sinners who trust in Him.

The Prophets Longed to See It

Peter highlights the worth of our salvation by telling us how the prophets longed to be a part of it. Verse 11: "The prophets who prophesied of the grace that would come to you made careful search and inquiry, seeking to know what person or time [Christ was indicating]."

Christ came to Isaiah 700 years before the incarnation and instructed him to write —

> He was wounded for our transgressions; he was bruised for our iniquities; the chastisement of our peace was upon him, and with

his stripes we are healed. All we like sheep have gone astray; we have turned every one to his own way; and the LORD hath laid on him the iniquity of us all (Isaiah 53:5-6, KJV).

When the Spirit of Christ told Isaiah to write that, Isaiah said, "O, Lord, who? O, Lord, when?" How long, O Lord, how long?

That searching and inquiring and longing is an echo of the tremendous worth of our salvation in the hearts of the holy men of old.

If you'll permit me a brief aside here, this is the reason I struggle with the end times obsession in believers today. Though there is a great deal of popular fiction devoted to being "left behind" or "the rapture," it is fiction. Myth. The "rapture" is not in the Bible. I know that may get me in trouble with some people (some in my own family), but it is the truth. And though I don't have time or space to delve into that here, I will say that if the prophets of old couldn't understand what was to come, then I'm pretty sure these TV preachers spouting all this fiction today can't either. (Okay, rant over.)

The Prophets Served Us in It

The Lord's answer to that yearning cry of the prophets is given in 1 Peter 1:12, "It was revealed to them that they were not serving themselves, but you."

The Spirit of Christ may have said to Isaiah, "Isaiah, be patient, you aren't serving yourself or even merely your own generation. You are serving saints hundreds of years from now. They will see in your prophecy of Me the proof that I am who I say I am. And its truth will make its infinite value unshakable in their lives. You will not have lived in vain."

The Angels Love to Look into It

The next thing Peter says to highlight the value of our salvation is that angels love to look into it. See the end of verse 12: "things into which angels long to look." This does not mean they want to but can't. It means they want to because in a sense, they are outsiders to the drama of sin and redemption (since they never sinned), and they love to watch the great work of God's salvation unfold in history and in the lives of the saints.

Peter's point is this: If angels get excited about our salvation, how much more should we? If angels love to look at the work of God in saving sinners like us, how much more should we who are the beneficiaries of that salvation (not just onlookers) love to look into it and be thankful for it and say with Peter, "Blessed be the God and Father of our Lord Jesus Christ..."

The Holy Spirit Brings It to Us

Finally, Peter highlights the value of our salvation by telling us in verse 12 that the Holy Spirit Himself sent from heaven has brought us the news of our salvation through the gospel. "These things... now have been announced to you through those who preached the gospel to you by the Holy Spirit sent from heaven" (NASB).

This is the gospel, the good news that Christ came into the world to save sinners, with a salvation of tremendous value—far more valuable than anything else you own or know.

- A salvation that was searched and inquired by prophets for years.
- A salvation that has been known and planned since the dawn of time.
- A salvation prepared NOT for those prophets and heroes of the faith, but for you.
- A salvation that is an enthralling mystery... even to the celestial beings. Even angels long to be a part of this.

It is more important, more valuable, more central, more joyous and vital than ANYTHING... ANY... THING... you or I could look at, devote ourselves to, or be a part of.

It's easy for many of us today to feel like we don't matter — whether you are a senior citizen who feels marginalized by your church or a youth group member who feels like you are continually deemed too young. Sometimes you even feel invisible, but here's the part you need to hear. You are so vitally important that all those heroes you learned about in Sunday School, all those prophets, were put there to serve you. Those majestic angels that are so incredibly awesome that every time they appear people shudder in fear, those beings long to understand what God is doing . . . in you.

Yes, you.

You are that important. You are part of the fulfillment of the mystery of God. If that doesn't make you feel special . . . I don't know what will.

Discussion Questions

1. Tell about a time you felt inspired. What did it feel like? How did it work?

2. Why is it hard for people who have grown up in the church to see a need to truly be saved?

3. How does being saved FOR instead of saved FROM change your worldview as a Christian?

4. Why is it hard for us to celebrate the value of our salvation?

CHAPTER THREE

Girded for Grace

"There's something out there waiting for us, and it ain't no man. We're all gonna die."
— Billy — Predator

What's your first thought when you hear the phrase, "gird up your loins"?

What are some phrases we would use today that mean the same thing? "Man up? Saddle up? Get busy!" We could go on and on with this list.

Now read 1 Peter 1:13.

> "Therefore, preparing your minds for action, and being sober-minded, set your hope fully on the grace that will be brought to you at the revelation of Jesus Christ" (ESV).

That phrase translated, "preparing your minds for action" is literally "gird up the loins of your mind." So if you were a reader in the first century who was familiar with what "girding" is all about, what would you have thought Peter was communicating here?

ALIENATED

Girding up the loins is a biblical concept and is used many times in Scripture.

Elijah girded up his loins and outran Ahab's chariot from Carmel to Jezreel. God's hand was on Elijah, (1 Kings 18:41–46). Elisha told Gehazi to gird up his loins, take his staff and go quickly and heal the Shunammite's son, (2 Kings 4:29). Later, Elisha called one of the sons of the prophets and told him to gird up his loins, take a box of oil to Ramoth-gilead and anoint Jehu king of Israel, (2 Kings 9:1–3). God told Jeremiah to gird up his loins, arise and speak unto Judah all His words, (Jeremiah 1:17). Jeremiah acted out the type of the linen girdle on his loins, (Jeremiah 13:1, 2, 4, 11). And finally, God told Job: "Gird up your loins like a man; for I will demand of you, and answer thou me" (Job 38:3, 40:7).

But this is not merely a physical thing. Scripturally, you will find many admonitions to gird up your loins spiritually as well.

Of the Messiah, the Bible says, "righteousness shall be the girdle of His loins, and faithfulness the girdle of His reins" (Isaiah 11:5). The four living creatures Ezekiel saw had loins the appearance of fire (Ezekiel 1:27, 8:2). To Daniel, the angel's loins looked like fine gold (Daniel 10:5).

We are to take on the whole armor of God, "having your loins girded with truth" (Ephesians 6:13–18, NASB1995)

The Israelites in Egyptian slavery had to have their loins girded, ready to travel three days into the wilderness to sacrifice to the Lord.

A certain group of believers of the church of Laodicea think they have their loins girded and are ready, but actually are naked and bare, not ready for the Master's return(Revelation 3:14–22). As Israel of old waited with loins girded for the death angel to Passover and for the Lord to lead them out of Egyptian bondage, so we are to wait with loins girded for the Messiah's return.

Luke 12:31–48 summarizes our requirement:

Girded for Grace

> Let your loins be girded about, and your lights burning; And ye yourselves like unto men that wait for their lord, when he will return from the wedding; that when he cometh and knocketh, they may open unto him immediately. Blessed are those servants, whom the lord when he comes shall find watching (KJV).

So how exactly does one "gird up your loins?" That's something a modern reader doesn't truly get. Maybe a little explanation will help us understand Peter's meaning better.

Back in the days of the ancient Near East, both men and women wore flowing tunics. Around the tunic, they'd wear a belt or girdle. Although tunics were comfortable and breezy, the hem of the tunic would often get in the way when a man was fighting or performing hard labor. So, when ancient Hebrew men had to battle the Philistines, for example, the men would lift the hem of their tunic up and tuck it into their girdle or tie it in a knot to keep it off the ground. The effect basically created a pair of shorts that provided more freedom of movement. So the bottom line is to tell someone to "gird up their loins" was to tell them to get ready for hard work or battle. It was the ancient way of saying "man up!"

Though I've had a vague notion of what it meant to gird up your loins, I've always been curious how exactly you do it. If you are like me and you have ever wondered about the intricacies of "loin-girding," then you are in luck!

Below is a handy guide with step-by-step instructions for your enjoyment and edification. In case tunics ever come back in style, you'll now know how to gird up your loins and get ready for action.

Instructions for Girding Your Loins:

1. Since a tunic will not easily allow you to do heavy labor or fight in battle, certain modifications are necessary, thus the "girding" of one's loins.

2. First, hoist the tunic up so that all the fabric is above your knees. This will give you mobility.
3. Gather all the extra material in front of you, so that the back of the tunic is snug against your backside.
4. Once the excess fabric is gathered in front, pull it underneath and between your legs to your rear. (This feels much like a diaper.)
5. Gather half the material in each hand, bringing it back around to the front.
6. Finally, tie your two handfuls of material together, and you're all set for both battle and some hard labor.

In effect, this is a metaphorical way of saying, "Saddle up!" Get ready for action. Get ready to go to work.

When Peter uses the phrase, "gird up the loins of your mind," he is telling them to get their mind set up to go to war. Get your mind set to go to work.

Now read that verse again.

> "Therefore, preparing your minds for action, and being sober-minded, set your hope fully on the grace that will be brought to you at the revelation of Jesus Christ" (1 Peter 1:13).

Peter has set the stage with a brilliant introduction, giving them the exceptional value of their salvation and encouraging his readers to be "born again" to a living hope. Now he's getting down to business. This is some of the nitty-gritty, how-to of Christian living. So you gotta "gird up the loins of your mind" and get ready to get down to business.

So that living hope that you have been born again into is set fully on the grace of Jesus Christ.

This is where a lot of people struggle. We love to sing about "Amazing Grace," but we struggle mightily with it. Why do you think we struggle with grace so much?

Grace is unmerited favor. It is undeserved. It is unearned.

Grace is NOT cheap. It is free to the recipient, but to the giver, grace is always costly.

We are suspicious of anything "free." There always has to be a catch. We are too independent. We hate being indebted. We want control.

We prefer v. 14–16 much more than we do anything that talks about "grace." As obedient children, do not be conformed to the passions of your former ignorance, but as he who called you is holy, you also be holy in all your conduct, since it is written, "You shall be holy, for I am holy."

You are aliens. You are not of this world. You live here but you are different. A new creation.

THEREFORE, focus on the grace of Jesus. That's your hope. That's where your mind is. Focus on the grace of Jesus rather than on the desires of your old self.

When you do that, you will be set apart. Different. HOLY.

Too often, we read the word *holy* as *perfect*. We think God is calling us to be perfect. That is not the case. The word here, *hagion* is literally a word that means "set apart," "different," "other." In the New Testament, *hágios* ("holy") has the "technical" meaning "different from the world" because "like the Lord."

Peter is using a lot of words here that continue to convey to us an idea of being "different" and therefore "set apart" from the world around us.

Be different from the world as one who is alienated, living your life in fear.

> "And if you call on him as Father who judges impartially according to each one's deeds, conduct yourselves with fear throughout the time of your exile..." (1 Peter 1:17).

The word *fear* here has the literal connotation of "withdrawing" or "pulling away." Do you see the picture we're getting here?

Be holy (different and other) living in fear (pulling away) during your sojourning (journey through a strange land).

Peter is basically telling people, YOU DON'T BELONG HERE. SO QUIT ACTING LIKE YOU DO! GET RID OF ALL THE NONSENSE THAT ONCE MADE YOU A PART OF THIS WORLD AND BE DIFFERENT!

How then should we act like we belong in the world? In our lives? In our families? In our workplace? In our church?

Let's revisit 1 Peter 1:17 as well as the verses that follow.

> "And if you call on him as Father who judges impartially according to each one's deeds, conduct yourselves with fear throughout the time of your exile, knowing that you were ransomed from the futile ways inherited from your forefathers, not with perishable things such as silver or gold, but with the precious blood of Christ, like that of a lamb without blemish or spot (17–19).

Wait a minute . . . we hope in grace (which is unearned and undeserved), but God will judge us by our deeds (what we do). Does that make sense?

The word for "ransomed" is *lutroo* (pronounced lute — trow — oh), which literally means to restore to its rightful owner. You have been bought back. Paid for. Ransomed.

Not with money but with the precious blood of Christ. And THAT is why you live righteously.

Not in fear of judgment, but "pulling away" from the sin from which you have been released. The deeds that you are doing, those are passing on the unmerited favor of grace that you have so freely received.

Girded for Grace

You are God's. You were enslaved and captured by sin and death, but the blood of Christ bought you back. Now you are to be about the business of helping others enslaved and captured. You are to bring help. To bring relief. To lead them to salvation.

In Ernest Gordon's true account of life in a World War II Japanese prison camp, *Through the Valley of the Kwai*, there is a story that never fails to move me. It is about a man who through giving it all away literally transformed a whole camp of soldiers. The man's name was Angus McGillivray. Angus was a Scottish prisoner in one of the camps filled with Americans, Australians, and Britons who had helped build the infamous Bridge over the River Kwai. The camp had become an ugly situation. A dog-eat-dog mentality had set in. Allies would literally steal from one another and cheat each other; men would sleep on their packs yet have them stolen from under their heads.

Survival was everything. The law of the jungle prevailed . . . until the news of Angus McGillivray's death spread throughout the camp. Rumors spread in the wake of his death. No one could believe big Angus had succumbed. He was strong, one of those whom they had expected to be the last to die.

Actually, it wasn't the fact of his death that shocked the men, but the reason he died. Finally, they pieced together the true story.

The Argylls (Scottish soldiers) took their buddy system seriously. Their buddy was called their "mucker," and these Argylls believed that is was literally up to each of them to make sure their "mucker" survived. Angus's mucker, though, was dying, and everyone had given up on him, everyone, of course, but Angus. He had made up his mind that his friend would not die. Someone had stolen his mucker's blanket. So Angus gave him his own, telling his mucker that he had "just come across an extra one." Likewise, every mealtime, Angus would get his rations and take them to his friend, stand over him and force him to eat them, again stating that he was able to get "extra food." Angus was going to do anything and everything to see that his buddy got what he needed to recover.

But as Angus's mucker began to recover, Angus collapsed, slumped over, and died. The doctors discovered that he had died of starvation complicated by exhaustion. He had been giving of his own food and shelter. He had given everything he had — even his very life. The ramifications of his acts of love and unselfishness had a startling impact on the compound.

> "Greater love has no one than this, that a person will lay down his life for his friends" (John 15:12, NASB).

As word circulated of the reason for Angus McGillivray's death, the feel of the camp began to change. Suddenly, men began to focus on their mates, their friends, and humanity of living beyond survival, of giving oneself away. They began to pool their talents — one was a violin maker, another an orchestra leader, another a cabinet maker, another a professor. Soon the camp had an orchestra full of homemade instruments and a church called the "Church Without Walls" that was so powerful and compelling, even the Japanese guards attended. The men began a university, a hospital, and a library system. The place was transformed; an all but smothered love revived, all because one man named Angus gave all he had for his friend. For many of those men, this turnaround meant survival. What happened is an awesome illustration of the potential unleashed when one person actually gives it all away.

So how do the alienated live in this strange land? Not according to the futile ways of their fathers, not according to the mores of the world, but in love. A love that finds its hope in grace and its deeds in extending that grace to a lost and dying world.

That's hard for us to hear today. We get so bogged down in whatever is going on: family, life, bills, careers, finances, politics, even good works that we have a hard time acting like we don't belong here. In fact, the perception of the world is increasingly that Christians are not that different from everyone else anyway. We are just as judgmental, just as condescending, just as hypocritical as anyone else who is a part of this world.

Whenever we turn on the news and see a group of people picketing the funeral of dead soldiers because they profess hatred of their God for a group of people caused the death and pain that this family is undergoing, there seems to be little set apart or holy about such a display.[1] But because these things are supposedly done in the name of Jesus, this is the picture that many in our culture have of us as believers.

So Peter, what does it look like to live this alienated life? What does it look like to be "different" and "other" "pulling away" during this "journey through a strange land"?

Having purified your souls by your obedience to the truth for a sincere brotherly love, love one another earnestly from a pure heart, since you have been born again, not of perishable seed but of imperishable, through the living and abiding word of God (1 Peter 1:22–23, ESV). Peter's answer? Love!

Love is an action. Love is active. Now, I know what you're thinking... I've seen all the Julia Roberts movies, and they all tell me that love is a feeling. But that isn't a biblical view of love. Love is not a feeling or a fleeting emotion that comes and goes in relation to how I feel about you at a given moment. Love is a choice. Love is an action.

We've tried to teach our daughters that. Sometimes, Hilary is at work, and while I'm home with the girls, and I'll fold clothes or do dishes or something. One of them will ask, "Daddy, why do you have to do that NOW? Why can't it wait till Mommy gets home?" And I'll answer, "Well, sometimes I say I love you by doing things. Anybody

---

[1] Holy Sweat, Tim Hansel, 1987, Word Books Publisher, pp. 146–147

ALIENATED

can say those words, but clean dishes, folded laundry or a mopped floor sometimes say it a lot better." Because we know love is an action.

Luke tells the story of Jesus' commands to love a little differently than the others. Instead of just giving commands, he fleshes them out.

> And behold, a lawyer stood up to put him to the test, saying, "Teacher, what shall I do to inherit eternal life?" He said to him, "What is written in the Law? How do you read it?" And he answered, "You shall love the Lord your God with all your heart and with all your soul and with all your strength and with all your mind, and your neighbor as yourself." And he said to him, "You have answered correctly; do this, and you will live" (Luke 10:25-28).

Did you catch that? What are the secrets of eternal life? Love God. Love people. Wow!

> But he, desiring to justify himself, said to Jesus, "And who is my neighbor?" Jesus replied, "A man was going down from Jerusalem to Jericho, and he fell among robbers, who stripped him and beat him and departed, leaving him half dead. Now by chance a priest was going down that road, and when he saw him he passed by on the other side. So likewise a Levite, when he came to the place and saw him, passed by on the other side. But a Samaritan, as he journeyed, came to where he was, and when he saw him, he had compassion. He went to him and bound up his wounds, pouring on oil and wine. Then he set him on his own animal and brought him to an inn and took care of him. And the next day he took out two denarii and gave them to the innkeeper, saying, 'Take care of him, and whatever more you spend, I will repay you when I come back.' Which of these three, do you think, proved to be a neighbor to the man who fell among the robbers?" He said, "The one who

showed him mercy." And Jesus said to him, "You go, and do likewise" (Luke 10:29–37).

Jesus unlocks the third part of our mission with this story. We've heard this so much that the story has become common to us. Our familiarity causes us to miss some of the shock of the story.

Jesus asks the man to define which one was the neighbor, and Jesus defined that by *action*. Not by religiousness. Not by self-righteousness.

Not by their birthright, pedigree, or tribe. But by what they DID. Love is an action.

To love our neighbors. To love in action. To love through service.

You might hear a lot of talk about the most important thing for a church. Is it how we worship? Is it the preaching? Is it the correct doctrine? Is it the name on the building?

I would submit to you it's none of those things. It's *love*.

Think about Matthew 25. it's the ONLY place in the Bible where we get a picture of judgment from someone who actually knows what it's going to look like. And what is the criteria for judgment? Is it what fellowship you attended?

Is it how you worshiped? Is it your ratio of church attendance? No. It is based on *how* you loved. How you showed that love. How you fed, clothed, visited, and served those around you.

It's all about love.

If we can get that, the whole thing changes.

Discussion Questions

1. What are some idioms we use today that are reflective of "gird up your loins?"
2. For what are we to be girding our loins? How does that affect you personally? Your church?

ALIENATED

3. How does the idea of being ransomed change our understanding of our own salvation?

4. Peter says love is the answer. Paul will say that love is greater than faith and hope. How does this play out in our lives? In our churches?

CHAPTER FOUR

Building Blocks

"If the government is covering up knowledge of aliens, they're doing a better job of it than they are of anything else."
— **Stephen Hawking**

So put away all malice and all deceit and hypocrisy and envy and all slander. Like newborn infants, long for the pure spiritual milk, that by it you may grow up into salvation — if indeed you have tasted that the Lord is good. As you come to him, a living stone rejected by men but in the sight of God chosen and precious . . . (1 Peter 2:1–4, ESV).

Live in LOVE. Love each other earnestly from a pure heart, not for what you can get out of it or for yourself, but loving like Jesus.

This world doesn't work that way. This world works on malice, deceit, hypocrisy, envy, and slander.

Don't believe me? Log into social media. (Not right now, put the phone away.) Social media shows you the culture in which we live. We see the dark underbelly of much of our consumer culture portrayed vividly in our interactions online.

It's a culture of malice — badness, wickedness, evil (translated malice)

It's a culture of deceit — (guile) meaning decoy, to trick, to bait and switch; deceitfulness, trickery.

It's a culture of hypocrisy — (hypocrisy) acting under a feigned part, pretending, fakeness.

It's a culture of envy — (envy) ill-will, jealousy, spite.

It's a culture of slander — (evil words) backbiting, defamation, talking bad about others.

A while back, I saw posts on social media put up by sweet saintly souls that were members of the body I was serving at the time. They were vicious in their attack on political figures. They were also filled with things that had already been proven to be patently untrue. When I spoke to one of these sweet ladies about from where such a post could have come, they replied, "Well, it doesn't matter if it's true or not because it COULD be true!" Another said, "Those people did the same thing to some of our leaders. So, we have to give them a taste of their own medicine!"

Wait, what? I'm pretty sure that "it might be true" and "they did it first" are not acceptable reasons for behaving like the world. That doesn't sound like spiritually mature believers; it sounds like toddlers throwing a tantrum!

Peter says to put all that junk away. That's the stuff that drives this world, but love is what drives us.

Peter wraps up the first chapter with that statement. Loving one another with a pure brotherly love. Loving one another earnestly from a pure heart. Loving one another because you have been reborn of imperishable seed.

That seed is the living and abiding word of God. That word is the gospel, the good news that was preached to you.

When we get rid of all that junk, then we grow up — we're weaned, to use Peter's illustration here. And we come to Jesus.

That's sometimes hard for us to grasp. We want to believe that theological discussion or doctrinal debate are marks of spiritual maturity. We want to believe that those who can focus on the intricacies of Scripture are the ones who are more mature. Peter, however, says that growing up into salvation involves a repentance.

Repentance is not merely a necessity for high-profile sinners. Every person is a sinner, and every sinner must repent. Repentance is mandatory for kings and presidents, rulers and common folk. It is for popes and priests, ministers and pastors, elders and deacons, fathers and mothers, sons and daughters. The hardened criminal is no more in need of repentance than any other sinner. Remember after Hurricane Katrina, there were "Christian leaders" who opined that God had brought this disaster on New Orleans because they were somehow worse than all the rest of us. More recently, during the pandemic, there were leaders who preached that the virus was somehow a judgment from God. There is something hypocritical about concluding that the subjects of calamity are somehow greater sinners than the rest of us and in greater need of repentance.

If nothing else, it is evident from Paul's rebuke to the Romans that all of us need to understand the specific purpose of the goodness of God is to lead us to repentance: "Or do you show contempt for the riches of his kindness, forbearance and patience, not realizing that God's kindness is intended to lead you to repentance?" (Romans 2:4, NIV).

Repentance is mandatory. It is essential. It is tied to forgiveness and is an integral part of our salvation. Yet we have relegated it to simply saying, "Sorry." It is so much more than that. I think there are people who call themselves Christian who have never truly repented, and that is something that we must, as a church, speak into our world.

Walter Scott's five-finger exercise was originally a six-point mirror. Three of the points related to us and three related to God.

Faith, Repentance, Baptism — Us
Forgiveness, Holy Spirit, Eternal Life — God

He winnowed it down to believe, repent, be baptized for forgiveness of sins, the gift of the Holy Spirit, and eternal life. Somewhere along the way, it was transformed into a checklist of things that I do, and God's part was sort of removed from the whole deal.

Scott would later regret this misunderstanding of his message. Fred Craddock will later write of Scott: "This man, who understood repentance not as just a feeling, not standing paralyzed in a pool of pity but reformation of life — mind and body and will — and demonstrating such by acts of charity, benevolence, generosity, honesty, and dependability."

Scott himself would write later in his life in 1838, looking back on the work he, Campbell, and Stone had done offered, "We may have recovered the original gospel, but we have not yet got to the root of the evil."

Repentance is a vital part of our salvation, our forgiveness, and our relationship with God. May He bless our study and draw us into a straight path of relationship with Him.

Repentance is about turning away. It's an ongoing act of putting away all the things of the world, the things that we once lived in, and turning wholeheartedly toward God. That's what Peter is talking about at the beginning of chapter two. Putting away all these things of the world and craving the nourishment of the Word that causes us to grow up. That "growing up" actually helps us to be built up.

As we come to the living stone that was rejected by men, we, too, are becoming living stones. Building blocks that are building a new house, a new tabernacle, a new temple where a holy priesthood will offer spiritual sacrifices to God:

". . . you yourselves like living stones are being built up as a spiritual house, to be a holy priesthood, to offer spiritual sacrifices acceptable to God through Jesus Christ" (1 Peter 2:5).

That culture, alienated and set apart from the world, is being built up into a new creation. We call that creation "church."

There's a story about a king of Sparta in ancient Greece who boasted to a visiting monarch about the mighty walls of Sparta, but the guest looked around and didn't see any walls. Finally, he said to his host, "I'd like to see those walls. Show them to me!" The Spartan ruler pointed with great satisfaction to some disciplined and well-trained troops, part of Sparta's mighty army, and exclaimed, "There they are! Those are the walls of Sparta!"

Just as each Spartan soldier was viewed by the king as a brick in his mighty wall, so we are viewed by God as "living stones . . . built up a spiritual house."

You see, you are the church. Not any bricks or mortar, Peter says that you are the living stones that are formed together by God into a spiritual house. The people of the church are you and I.

That's sometimes hard for us to understand, and that's partly because of our own Bibles.

Here's why: The word *church* is not scriptural.

Stay with me. Part of the problem with our mindset is because of the Bibles we read.

When I was growing up, the only acceptable Bible you could read was the King James Version. I've even had church members at places I've served say to me, "If the King James was good enough for Paul, then it's good enough for me!"

The King James is a good translation . . . for the time it was originally published. The King James translators did a good job with the resources they had.

Unfortunately, they didn't have all the tools they needed at their disposal.

Many times, they were translating from a translation of a translation of a translation. A lot of times, they were working from a Latin text instead of the original language. And they did the best they could.

However, since that time, we have uncovered a ton of manuscripts. There are a lot more tools available now than there were at the time of King James, and ... we don't have to filter through some of the kings and bishops with whom they had to work.

Sometimes, those translations were at the mercy of the church they were serving. Unfortunately, church, just like any other bureaucracy, would strive to keep itself alive.

The original word that we read as *church* today is *ekklesia*. Literally this means "an assembly of those called out." So "the assembly" or "the called out" is how the translators rendered that word.

But church leaders were worried that this was divisive. If you tell people to be "called out," then there's a chance they will be called out of the church's control. You don't want people thinking that they can be called out away from the establishment. So, they changed the word.

He had them insert the word *church* everywhere *ekklesia* was used (except for the times when it's used to describe an angry mob). The word *church* means a located chapel, so it changed a lot of the meaning behind phrases in Scripture.

For example: We, in churches of Christ, take our name from Romans 16:16 — Greet one another with a holy kiss. The churches of Christ greet you (ESV).

A phrase that would have originally been understood to be "All those called out by Christ" now becomes a sign on the side of a building describing a specific place.

We understand, though, that the church has nothing at all to do with a sign on the side of a pile of bricks. Instead the church is a "spiritual house" that is built out of "living stones." Those stones are you and I. The church is the people.

> "But you are a chosen race, a royal priesthood, a holy nation, a people for his own possession, that you may proclaim the excellencies of him who called you out of darkness into his marvelous light. Once you were not a people, but now you are God's people; once you had not received mercy, but now you have received mercy" (1 Peter 2:9–10).

That spiritual house is being built to proclaim the excellencies of Him. That's why we're here. We are not here to be a moral compass. We are not here to bring morality to our nation. We are not here to grow ourselves or to protect a denomination.

We are built to proclaim to a lost, dark, and dying world the power, glory, and goodness of our Lord. Period. We are here to tell the world how wonderful, gracious and loving our God is. We are here to praise and glorify His holy name. That's our purpose.

The church is the plan of God to spread the story of salvation to a lost and dying world. There is not a "plan B." The church is what it is all about.

We all need to live for something bigger than ourselves. Paul David Tripp writes in his book, *A Quest for More*, "There is woven inside each of us a desire for something more — a craving to be part of something bigger, greater, and more profound than our relatively meaningless day-to-day existence."[2] That longing to be part of something more in your life — that's God-given.

---

[2] Tripp, Paul David. *A Quest for More*. New Growth Press, 2008.

That's why, regardless of what cause you champion, it is worthless in comparison to the ministry of the gospel of Jesus Christ. That is why you belong in church.

The church is God's plan, God's design, God's means of revealing this great mystery to the world.

You can waste your life in the false peace of worldly comfort and small ambition and being cool. You can waste your time on politics, causes and worldly pursuits. Or you can be a part of something eternal.

Jesus is looking for those who want to get messy and relevant and involved. He wants to use you for the advance of the gospel. Don't miss out. Don't settle for a life that won't matter forever. Do you want people to say at your funeral, "What a nice person!" and that's it? Your life can count for many people forever. All He asks of you, all you can do, is keep listening to Him moment by moment and then take the next step. You provide your weakness and need. He provides His strength, His wisdom, everything. If we will live that way on mission together, we will experience what only God can do.

God uses ordinary people, but what He does with them is extraordinary.

Paul loves to address this in his letters. One place where he speaks directly to the mission of the church is in Ephesians 3:

> "His intent was that now, through the church, the manifold wisdom of God should be made known to the rulers and authorities in the heavenly realms, according to his eternal purpose that he accomplished in Christ Jesus our Lord" (Ephesians 3:10-11, NIV).

This is going to blow our minds. The very existence of the church, Paul wrote, has a much higher purpose than we realize. It's an amazing thing that spiritually dead people are raised to new life and that former enemies become family with one another within the church. This is such a big deal that it is the way that God has chosen to reveal His wisdom in its rich variety.

Think for a minute of all the ways that God could show that He is wise. The human genome shows that God is wise. Scientists are unravelling all the ways information is stored in our DNA that makes us who we are. It's amazing! The universe shows God's wisdom. I could think of many ways that God could choose to show His wisdom, but look at how God has chosen to reveal His wisdom: through the church.

The church is God's chosen means for revealing this mystery, His wisdom.

There is no backup plan. There is no "Well, if this doesn't work, we can always do this." The church, you and me, are God's plan — and not just for a lost and dying world.

Paul says God is using you and me, in the church, to reveal this mystery to all creation. God is using the church to reveal His wisdom to all those being in the heavenly places.

See, Paul teaches us that there is a spiritual world that we cannot see. That world has a hierarchy, a rank. He says that God uses the church to reveal His wisdom to all those heavenly beings. That word translated as "rulers" means the ones who give the orders. The next word, translated as "authorities" are the ones who carry out those orders.

This is not simply some basic instruction for any spirit that might want to listen. No, class is in session, and the God of the universe is educating all the heavenly host.

The forces of evil believed that they had killed Jesus once and for all. When the Son of God, the Logos, the Word comes and walks among men, there must be a great plan of God unfolding. So, how do you stop such a plan? You kill Him. They did, but it didn't end there.

They had him in the tomb. All His followers were hiding and on the run. It was a complete victory. Then he rose from the dead and left.

It should be easy enough. This ragtag group of disciples never had amounted to much. In fact, they could barely keep on track while they had Jesus with them. They never seemed to understand what He was trying to tell them. Not one of them ever demonstrated any type of bravery or leadership, but then, things began to happen. Peter — the same Peter who denied even knowing Him — rose to preach. He loudly proclaimed Jesus as the Messiah. Though thrown in jail and threatened with death, he never backed down.

Thousands joined the church. It became an unstoppable movement. The forces of darkness continued to do everything in their power to stop the spread of this gospel, but the church just continued to grow. Throughout Judea and on into the greater Roman Empire, this ragtag group led an ever-growing congregation of the marginalized to become the most dominant religious force in most of the known world!

This great cosmic production played out on the global world stage as churches became the leading actors. The play is written by the hand of God, and under His perfect direction, the story continues to unfold.

The audience is not the world. The audience is not the church. The audience is the powers and principalities, the angels, and the entire heavenly host. They are spectators in the great dramatic story of creation, fall, and salvation. The story of the church of Jesus Christ becomes the greatest school for spiritual beings in the heavenly realm!

The church is evidence of the defeat of the forces of darkness. Those powers and authorities are put on notice that their power and authority has been destroyed and the end is near. God claims victory and proclaims through the church that the end of their reign is upon them.

God has chosen the church, of all things, to display His great wisdom on a cosmic scale!

That means that your church, big or small, is serving as a lesson for beings in the spiritual realm. We, with all our struggles and faults, become a tangible reminder that all authority on heaven and earth belongs to Jesus. He is victorious and has never stopped working within this world. The good news of that victory will never be stopped. God is at work in this world, and He is using us — you and me and all the other weird and wonderful saints in your congregation — as proof that His kingdom is forever victorious.

That is why you belong in a church.

Church is not just a social club or a political party. Church is not a social justice movement. Church is not just a place to make you feel comfortable until you can go to heaven. It is so much more than that.

The church of Jesus Christ is the single most important grouping of people in the history of the world! These children of God are more important and more world-changing than any other group, nation, or organization in world history. The United States is an insignificant speck in comparison to the glowing sun of the church. There is no comparison between the church of Jesus Christ and any human endeavor ever.

This is something the church needs to hear. You belong to a glorious victorious army of the Lord. You are part of a kingdom that will never die. You are the chosen, the beloved, the true love of the God of creation. You are the blood-bought precious bride of the risen Christ!

That brother who annoys you at church is part of the grand cosmic plan to educate the host of heaven. That sister who won't get out of your business is, in fact, a part of the body of the risen Christ proclaiming victory to the cosmos.

We live our lives with little or no awareness of the cosmic significance of our lives and this church.

Your gifts may not be huge, and your life may seem insignificant. That isn't the case.

It's part of something bigger, and it's part of the mission and plan of God in the world today.

Don't ever think that God can't use you. His power is made perfect in your weakness. How do you participate in God's plan? Get into a church, be a living part of that body, go deeper into the gospel, get involved and active in the mission and vision of the church. Then disciple someone else to do the same.

You belong. You were called to belong. You were made to belong.

You belong in a body. You belong in a family. You belong in church.

Peter pulls it all together with this statement: You are different, you are aliens, you are journeying through a foreign land . . . and as you do . . . stay away from those desires that you once lived in because they are waging war against your soul. He did not say that you would be bringing glory to God by your theology. This is not a statement that you would be glorifying God by going to church every Sunday. He said that you are to keep your conduct (what you do, how you live) out there in the world honorable so that people will see your good deeds (what you do, how you live) and glorify God.

It isn't about my knowing more Bible than the guy next to me. It isn't about whether I sat on the front row every Sunday for Bible class. It isn't about if I voted for the correct political party or whether I supported the correct cause or charity. It's about what I do. It's about living in love.

Peter says that we are to live in love. Be that holy temple of God, that holy nation, that royal priesthood that lives in love and works in love. Be the people who are so different from this fallen world they live in that those around may see the things we do in love and glorify God.

That's why we're here.

Discussion Questions

1. How does loving like Jesus change the face of a world that is so against anything that seems loving?

2. How do you see social media being a picture of the culture in which we truly reside?

3. Describe ways you have seen the church actually living as those "set apart" rather than merely being a "located chapel"?

4. How does the description of repentance presented here differ from our traditional understanding?

CHAPTER FIVE

Alien Behavior

"(Antarctica) is a very alien environment. And you can't survive here more than minutes if you aren't equipped properly and doing the right thing all the time."
— John Krakauer

Keep your conduct among the Gentiles honorable, so that when they speak against you as evildoers, they may see your good deeds and glorify God on the day of visitation.

Be subject for the Lord's sake to every human institution, whether it be to the emperor as supreme, or to governors as sent by him to punish those who do evil and to praise those who do good. For this is the will of God, that by doing good you should put to silence the ignorance of foolish people. Live as people who are free, not using your freedom as a cover-up for evil, but living as servants of God. Honor everyone. Love the brotherhood. Fear God. Honor the emperor (1 Peter 2:12–17, ESV).

I believe, contrary to how your version has edited it, that this section begins in verse 12. Verse 12 is almost the thesis statement for everything that Peter is going to say about submission.

Remember, he is speaking to people he calls aliens who are strangers, exiles, and sojourners in a foreign land. They are not at home. They are accused, persecuted, cursed, scoffed at, rejected, and vilified. In many ways, their world gives us a picture of where a non-Christian culture like ours is headed.

Increasingly, in our culture, Christians feel marginalized. Now, don't misunderstand me, a craft store being told to provide health insurance for its employees or a bakery forced to bake a cake for a customer is not persecution. It is, however, the beginning of that marginalization.

If we understand the timing and dating correctly, Peter was writing this during the time or near the time of Nero who was an emperor of Rome. He despised Christians and Christianity. He made it his mission to wipe out Christianity from the face of the earth. Nero reportedly burned the whole city to the ground and then blamed the Christians. This man dipped Christians in oil and set them on fire, still alive, to light his garden. That is persecution.

And what does Peter say to those who live under such a government? Be subject. Submit. Be good citizens.

But Peter . . . we protest . . . how do we reach the world around us? How do we share our faith with a lost and dying world? The same way Peter tells his alien readers in First Peter — by our lives.

> "Keep your conduct among the Gentiles honorable, so that when they speak against you as evildoers, they may see your good deeds and glorify God on the day of visitation" (1 Peter 2:12).

THEN HE SKIPS DOWN

> "For this is the will of God, that by doing good you should put to silence the ignorance of foolish people" (v. 15).

Alien Behavior

A few years ago, I saw a pastor posting on Facebook how he really wanted to go to the White House and assault the President. I laughed and thought, *I wonder what Peter would have to say about that*. I'm pretty sure I know. Peter would say to live honorable lives, do good deeds, and live for Jesus.

Over the past few years, we witnessed many Christians fighting with one another and the world around them over masks. The right to wear or not to wear a mask was a dividing issue. Are you, like me, wondering what Peter would say? I think when we read this, we know.

Behavior matters. Actions speak louder. Preach with your life.

Peter goes on to address those who are living as slaves or bondservants. Many of these Jews and Gentile believers were dispersed because they had been carried off with the household in which they were servants. They didn't have a choice but to go off into this foreign land. They were taken.

> Servants, be subject to your masters with all respect, not only to the good and gentle but also to the unjust. For this is a gracious thing, when, mindful of God, one endures sorrows while suffering unjustly. For what credit is it if, when you sin and are beaten for it, you endure? But if when you do good and suffer for it you endure, this is a gracious thing in the sight of God (1 Peter 2:18–20).

Behavior matters. Actions speak louder. Preach with your life.

We don't preach the faith in a God that comes by force and grinds you into submission. We preach the faith in a God who made Himself into one of us and humbled Himself. He made Himself nothing. He holds all the power in the universe, yet He used that power to become an infant.

Peter says that sure, you may have to suffer. But that's what we are called to in Jesus Christ. Why should we expect to be treated better than our Lord?

> For to this you have been called, because Christ also suffered for you, leaving you an example, so that you might follow in his steps. He committed no sin, neither was deceit found in his mouth. When he was reviled, he did not revile in return; when he suffered, he did not threaten, but continued entrusting himself to him who judges justly. He himself bore our sins in his body on the tree, that we might die to sin and live to righteousness. By his wounds you have been healed. For you were straying like sheep, but have now returned to the Shepherd and Overseer of your souls (1 Peter 2:21–25).

Jesus is the model. Jesus is the focus. We are all striving to be more like Him. And that's the point.

Jesus didn't tell us He loved us. He didn't give us a book with stories of His love. He showed us.

In the Broadway play, *My Fair Lady*, Eliza is courted by a man named Freddy. Freddy writes her love letters every day, but Eliza's response to all of these written promises is to cry out in frustration in the song, "Show Me."

I believe this is Peter's cry as well. Behavior matters. Actions speak. Preach with your life.

That's the example of Jesus. He showed us His love.

> "This is how we know what love is: Jesus Christ laid down his life for us. And we ought to lay down our lives for our brothers and sisters" (1 John 3:16, NIV).

Many commentators stop here. Then they pick up in chapter 3. But that doesn't work. Peter is not stopping here. This is all one big section regardless of how it's broken up in your Bible. Peter is going to go on and connect here with a single word: likewise.

> Likewise, wives, be subject to your own husbands, so that even if some do not obey the word, they may be won without a word by the conduct of their wives, when they see your respectful and pure conduct. Do not let your adorning be external — the braiding of hair and the putting on of gold jewelry, or the clothing you wear — but let your adorning be the hidden person of the heart with the imperishable beauty of a gentle and quiet spirit, which in God's sight is very precious. For this is how the holy women who hoped in God used to adorn themselves, by submitting to their own husbands, as Sarah obeyed Abraham, calling him lord. And you are her children, if you do good and do not fear anything that is frightening (1 Peter 3:1-6).

Honestly, I almost stopped here, too. Why? Well, I'm not the guy to write a book about telling women to submit. I live in a house with three women. I am totally outnumbered! As long as my wife is not around, I'll be the first to tell the glory of my authority in our house. I'm serious! I am totally in control and authority in our house... as long as it's all right with her.

Seriously though, these verses have been used along with a couple of others from Ephesians and Colossians to subjugate and abuse women for years.

And that totally isn't what Peter is talking about.

However, to fully understand this passage and this whole section of Scripture, we need to back up and look around a little bit.

I've heard people say that we "read too much into Scripture." They think we should just take it at face value, and that isn't a bad idea. The problem is that none of us is capable of doing that. We all come to Scripture with our baggage: preconceived beliefs, ideas, and cultural influences.

When we read a passage like this one, we overlay our Western, Americanized lenses upon it and say that it means something that it doesn't. To fully understand a passage like this, we must ask a few questions, beginning with, "In what context was this written?"

To understand this, we must know the viewpoint of those being addressed, meaning we must first understand the Greco-Roman "household codes."

As far back as the fourth century BC, philosophers considered the household to be a microcosm, designed to reflect the hierarchal structure of the society, the gods, and ultimately the universe. Aristotle wrote that "the smallest and primary parts of the household are master and slave, husband and wife, father and children." First-century philosophers Philo and Josephus included the household codes in their writings as well, arguing that a man's authority over his household was critical to the success of a society. Many Roman officials believed the household codes to be such an important part of Pax Romana that they passed laws ensuring its protection.

Biblical passages about wives submitting to their husbands are not, as many Christians assume, rooted in a culture epitomized by June Cleaver's kitchen, but in a culture epitomized by the Greco-Roman household codes, which gave men unilateral authority over their wives, slaves, and adult children. The apostles advocated this system not because God had revealed it as the divine will for Christian homes, but because it was the only stable and respectable system anyone knew about. It was the best the culture had to offer.

With Roman officials looking for every excuse to imprison Christians, challenging the codes would have brought even more unwanted scrutiny to the early Church. Behavior matters.

Though many who disagree will accuse us of allowing cultural norms to shape our views of gender roles, in this case, it seems it is those who hold to the past who have given culture — that of the Greco-Roman familial structure — the final word.

What about Paul's comparison of the submission of the wife to her husband to the relationship between Christ and the Church? Here's where it gets really cool: Though following a similar organizational structure, the household codes found in the Bible's epistles differ significantly from the household codes found in the pagan literature of the day. In a sense, they present us with a sort of Christian remix of Greco-Roman morality that attempts to preserve the apostle Paul's earlier teaching that "there is neither Jew nor Gentile, neither slave nor free, nor is there male and female, for you are all one in Christ Jesus" (Galatians 3:28, NIV).

Although typical Greco-Roman household codes required nothing of the head of household regarding fair treatment of subordinates, Peter and Paul encouraged men to be kind to their slaves, to be gentle with their children, and, shockingly, to love their wives as they love themselves. Furthermore, the Christian versions of the household codes are the only ones that speak directly to the less powerful members of the household — the slaves, wives, and children — probably because the church at the time consisted of just such powerless people.

To dignify their positions, Peter linked the sufferings of slaves to the suffering of Christ and likened the obedience of women to the obedience of Sarah (1 Peter 2:18–25; 3:1–6). Paul encourages slaves and women to submit the head of the household as "unto the Lord," reminding both slaves and their masters that they share a heavenly Master who shows no partiality in bestowing eternal inheritance (Ephesians 5:22; 6:5).

> "Likewise, husbands, live with your wives in an understanding way, showing honor to the woman as the weaker vessel, since they are

heirs with you of the grace of life, so that your prayers may not be hindered" (1 Peter 3:7).

I cannot overstate the degree to which this remix — in which masters are reminded that they too have a heavenly master — would have been radical in the ancient world. What's more, it placed responsibility rather than mere privilege, on the man of the house; responsibility for the slave to be treated as the suffering Christ and responsibility to hold the wife up as a weaker vessel. Now hear that! It isn't some declaration of who can bench press the most. It is the difference between a porcelain vase and an iron kettle! Sure, the iron kettle is stronger, but that porcelain vase is way more valuable. Weaker does not necessarily connote any type of diminished value. This is not calling men to come home, kick off their boots, and demand their woman to wait on them. If anything, it is taking that norm in the Greco-Roman codes and turning it on its ear. You, men, are responsible for the treatment of your slaves, your children, and your wives. You are responsible for holding up your wife as more valuable than yourself. You bear the responsibility that your treatment of her directly affects your relationship with God all the way to His receptiveness to your prayers.

This was gospel! This was good news! This was not abusive or subjugating or demeaning. This is not about chauvinism or misogyny. This is the radical freedom of those who are in Christ!

We must all submit to or to be in submission to God. That's the point that James makes when he writes in James 4:7 "Submit yourselves therefore to God. Resist the devil, and he will flee from you." The way James writes this is that being able to resist the devil is conditioned on whether we are submitting ourselves to God . . . only then will "he flee from you" but if you aren't submitting to God, you might not be able to resist the devil because you're resisting God. You can't expect God's help in resisting temptation from the devil or his demons while you're refusing to submit to Him. There is no guarantee that he will flee from you at all under this circumstance.

When Paul writes to the church at Rome that "the mind that is set on the flesh is hostile to God, for it does not submit to God's law; indeed, it cannot" (Romans 8:7), it is because it takes the Holy Spirit to be able to submit to God, not to mention to submit to His law. I think Paul is obviously speaking in Romans directly about the Ten Commandments, not the Mosaic Law. Those who don't have the Spirit of God are "being ignorant of the righteousness of God, and seeking to establish their own, they did not submit to God's righteousness" (Romans 10:3). This means that we are to submit to man's laws, too, at least when they don't conflict with the Laws of God. Paul writes, "Let every person be subject to the governing authorities.

For there is no authority except from God, and those that exist have been instituted by God" (Romans 13:1) and the reason is that "whoever resists the authorities resists what God has appointed, and those who resist will incur judgment" (Romans 13:2). This means we should "Pay to all what is owed to them: taxes to whom taxes are owed, revenue to whom revenue is owed, respect to whom respect is owed, honor to whom honor is owed" (Romans 13:7). That is godly submission. Resisting those in authority is resisting God Himself and if you aren't submitting to the laws of the land, you are not submitting to God. The reason that Israel was disciplined so often was that she "would not submit" to God (Psalm 81:11). Peter understood that we should "Be subject for the Lord's sake to every human institution, whether it be to the emperor as supreme, or to governors as sent by him to punish those who do evil and to praise those who do good" (1 Peter 2:13–14).

We typically don't think of submitting to one another in the church but only to those who are in authority over us. that isn't the case as Paul writes that we are to be "submitting to one another out of reverence for Christ" (Ephesians 5:21). This means we "serve one another humbly in love" (Galatians 5:13, NIV) and "in humility value others above yourselves" (Philippians 2:3), and as Peter tells the church, "clothe yourselves with humility toward one another, because, 'God opposes the proud but shows favor to the humble'" (1 Peter 5:5, NIV). Paul writes to the church at Corinth to be "subject to such as these, and to every fellow worker and laborer" (1 Corinthians 16:16), so submission isn't just for some; it is for all.

The Bible teaches that we should submit to one another out of a reverence for Christ, to esteem others better than ourselves, to obey those who have authority over us, and most of all, to submit ourselves under God's authority and His Law because God will resist all who refuse to submit and humble themselves but will only give grace to the humble, and humble people are submitting people.

> Finally, all of you, have unity of mind, sympathy, brotherly love, a tender heart, and a humble mind. Do not repay evil for evil or reviling for reviling, but on the contrary, bless, for to this you were called, that you may obtain a blessing. For
>
> "Whoever desires to love life and see good days,
>
> let him keep his tongue from evil and his lips from speaking deceit;
>
> let him turn away from evil and do good; let him seek peace and pursue it.
>
> For the eyes of the Lord are on the righteous, and his ears are open to their prayer.
>
> But the face of the Lord is against those who do evil."
>
> The eyes of the Lord are on the righteous, and his ears are open to their prayer (1 Peter 3:8–12).

Alien Behavior

Behavior matters.

Behavior matters in response to the authorities where you live. Behavior matters in the workplace.

Behavior matters in the home.

Behavior matters in how you relate to the unbeliever around you. And behavior matters in your relationship with God.

Ultimately, we don't like submission. We live in a culture that values individual freedom above all. Don't believe me? That's why we end up fighting about things like bathrooms, because the needs of the one outweigh the needs of the many. That's why we end up fighting about things like masks, because my rights outweigh the wants and needs of others.

Much of the time, we value the individual rights way more than we do anything else.

We don't like submitting. We don't like to be meek and humble. But the truth is; it isn't up to us.

A few years ago, I baptized a 91-year-old woman. She had been struggling with submission her whole life. She was raised independent and strong. She was a product of a hard, West Texas family that had always pulled themselves up by their own bootstraps and could not bring themselves to yield to anyone. But ultimately, it isn't up to us. We all submit. All the earth. Every one of us.

> "for it is written, 'As I live, says the Lord, every knee shall bow to me, and every tongue shall confess to God'" (Romans 14:11).

> "Therefore God exalted Him to the highest place, and gave him the name that is above every name, that at the name of Jesus every knee should bow, in heaven and on earth and under the earth, and every tongue acknowledge that Jesus Christ is Lord, to the glory of God the Father..." (Philippians 2:9–11, NIV).

We will all submit. One day we will all submit. But unlike a conquering king who comes in and demands submission or else; Jesus gives us the opportunity to offer submission as our sacrifice to Him.

Discussion Questions

1. Why is it so hard for us, especially Americans, to accept the idea of submission?
2. How have you seen the conduct or behavior of others change the way you viewed them?
3. How do Peter's directives to servants and masters carry over to the workplace today?
4. Why would Peter comparing servants to the suffering Christ be good news?
5. The "likewise" at the beginning of chapter 3 connects Peter's thoughts on husbands and wives with his words to servants. How are these two types of submission connected?
6. How do we show honor to things that might be perceived as weaker? (like a porcelain vase)

CHAPTER SIX

Alien Blood

"A person who is keen to see an alien should start practicing altruistic service to others and soon, most people will make him feel and realize that he is from a different planet."
— Anuj Somany

We are moving into 1 Peter 3, but first, turn over to John 2. I know, we're studying 1 Peter, but bear with me.

If you were God, if you were going to come to earth, if you were going to be God made flesh, if you were going to ransom your creation, how would you start?

First miracle, burst on the scene — grab the attention — let the world know things were about to change, what would you do?

Maybe part a sea? Remind them of Moses, ransoming the Israelites? That's a good one.

Maybe raise someone to life? Bring to mind Elijah or some of the prophets? If it's me, I want something big, right? Something that blows the mind.

Well, that wasn't what Jesus did. Jesus' first miracle was all about family and a party gone wrong.

> On the third day there was a wedding at Cana in Galilee, and the mother of Jesus was there. Jesus also was invited to the wedding with his disciples. When the wine ran out, the mother of Jesus said to him, "They have no wine." And Jesus said to her, "Woman, what does this have to do with me? My hour has not yet come." His mother said to the servants, "Do whatever he tells you" (John 2:1–5).

This is great! So, there's a wedding, and Mary is smack dab in the middle of it!

Now I know I'm reading into the text here, but humor me for a moment.

Mary seems like one of those folks who everyone else turns to for help. I know I'm making some assumptions, but I also think there are clues that bear me out. Think of all the things she has already endured in her life: the rumors, the gossip, the shaming. She, however, has emerged a strong woman. We see her strength and her personality a bit here in this story. There was a wedding, and Mary was there.

That's the way this story begins. There is a wedding happening, and the mother of Jesus is there!

She wasn't the only one though. Jesus and His disciples were invited, too. I love that in the beginning of this story, they are sort of an afterthought. They seem to be kind of a "by the way."

And then the unthinkable happens . . . the wine runs out.

This is not a faux pas. This is not an oops. This is a horrible embarrassment and will, in effect, ruin the entire wedding. In our society this is like, um, they dropped the entire wedding cake on the floor as they were setting it up, and there is none. Maybe even worse.

Alien Blood

When the wine ran out, the mother of Jesus said to Him, "They have no wine." And Jesus said to her, "Woman, what does this have to do with me? My hour has not yet come."

This is so beautiful. So human. So perfect.

Mary runs over to Jesus and says, "They're out of wine!" And He replies, "Not now."

Sometimes, I lie down at night and Hilary says, "I'm hot." Now when we were first married, I would say, "I'm sorry." Now that I speak her language a little better I understand that "I'm hot" means "Dear husband, would you go and turn the air down a bit?"

That's what happens here. Mary says, "They're out of wine." Now, because she's a mom, she *thinks* she said, "Go do something to fix this horrible problem."

He says, "Not now." We must understand that His use of the word *Woman* is not a dismissive term nor is it rude in any way; it's actually a term of endearment. We miss that because of the difference in language and not understanding the idioms of the culture. But the point of His response is, "Not now."

What does Mary do? She wasn't listening. She told the servants, "Do whatever He says." And then she is gone, back into the whirlwind of the wedding.

This leads me to believe that Mary must have been something of a personality. I mean, she was walking around, giving orders, and having servants jumping at her words. When she gave this servant a directive, he immediately responded. No questions. No consultations. He just followed the orders. She went on to say, "Do whatever He tells you to do." With that, she was gone.

When he said, "No," she heard, "Yes." Sound familiar? I have a mom, and this sounds completely familiar.

"Now there were six stone water jars there for the Jewish rites of purification, each holding twenty or thirty gallons. Jesus said to the servants, 'Fill the jars with water.' And they filled them up to the brim. And he said to them, 'Now draw some out and take it to the master of the feast.' So they took it" (John 2:6–8).

Now this is strange. This exchange makes you wonder because this is a weird segue. These jars are not where the wine was kept. Wine was kept in wineskins, which were skin bags made to hold wine. So why are we talking about these jars?

These jars were there to cleanse themselves ceremonially before a meal. Remember when the Pharisees got so mad because Jesus' disciples weren't washing their hands before eating? It wasn't about germs or hygiene; it was about ceremony. They would wash their hands, and as the water would run off, they would say this prayer. Then they would dip again, and as the water ran off, they would say a different prayer. It was a ceremony. It was about cleansing themselves. It was a ritual.

Halakha requires the hands to be washed before eating any type of meal containing bread. This washing was initially called *mayim rishonim* (first waters), but is now commonly known simply as *netilat yadayim* (hand washing).

This only applies to bread made from one of the five chief grains (wheat, cultivated barley, spelt, wild barley, and oats). The washing is performed by pouring water from a cup over each hand.

The Gemarah of the Babylonian Talmud contains homiletic descriptions of the importance of the practice, including an argument that washing before meals is so important that neglecting it is tantamount to unchastity or even adultery, and doing so risks divine punishment in the form of sudden destruction or poverty.

Rabbinic law requires that travelers go as far as four biblical miles to obtain water for washing prior to eating bread, if there is a known water source there. This applies only to when the water source lies in one's direction of travel. However, had he already passed the water source, he is only obligated to backtrack to one biblical mile. The one exception to this rule is when a man or a party of men are encamped while on a journey, and there is no water to be found in the vicinity of their camp. In such a case, the Sages of Israel have exempted them from washing their hands prior to breaking bread.

What does this ceremonial bathwater have to do with a wedding? Why are we talking about bath water?

Jesus tells the servants to fill these things up, so they do — somewhere in the neighborhood of 180 gallons. They filled them to the brim.

How would you like to be that servant? I mean this woman comes and grabs you and says, "Do what that guy tells you." And that guy? He says go fill up the bathwater. Now take a cup of that to your boss.

I wonder when the change happened. When did the water in the servant's hand actually change? Did it happen immediately when he dipped it out? Did it happen when they filled it up? Did it happen on the way to the Master of the feast? You know that servant had to be nervous.

> When the master of the feast tasted the water now become wine, and did not know where it came from (though the servants who had drawn the water knew), the master of the feast called the bridegroom and said to him, "Everyone serves the good wine first, and when people have drunk freely, then the poor wine. But you have kept the good wine until now." This, the first of his signs, Jesus did at Cana in Galilee, and manifested his glory. And his disciples believed in him (9-11).

I love that the miracle is kind of forgotten. I mean, no one says a word. Jesus doesn't get up and do some magical flourishes. He doesn't seek credit or accolades. The only people who even know something happened are His disciples and some servants. That's it!

ALIENATED

I think that's amazing! I don't wash a dish or sweep a floor at our house without having to get credit! I want the credit! I want it to be known that I did something! *Hey honey, look what I did!*

The focus here though is not on the miracle. This, John says, is the first of His signs. A sign of what? A sign of power? A sign of divinity? Or a sign that things were changing?

Gone is the holy bathwater. Jesus turns the ritual and ceremony into a party. There is no power, no holiness, no divinity in that water. It's just water. And in Jesus' kingdom . . . it's going to be different.

Turn back to 1 Peter. Let's look at chapter 3, verses 18–22:

> For Christ also suffered once for sins, the righteous for the unrighteous, that he might bring us to God, being put to death in the flesh but made alive in the spirit, in which he went and proclaimed to the spirits in prison, because they formerly did not obey, when God's patience waited in the days of Noah, while the ark was being prepared, in which a few, that is, eight persons, were brought safely through water. Baptism, which corresponds to this, now saves you, not as a removal of dirt from the body but as an appeal to God for a good conscience, through the resurrection of Jesus Christ, who has gone into heaven and is at the right hand of God, with angels, authorities, and powers having been subjected to him.

Scholars will call this one of the most confusing and difficult passages in the New Testament. There is much debate and argument over what Peter is talking about here.

For our purposes, I don't want to get bogged down in spirits in prison and what that means because I think we can tend to focus on that so much that we miss the point. There are much smarter guys than me writing much deeper analyses of those concerns. What I really want us to focus in on is verse 21:

Alien Blood

> "Baptism, which corresponds to this, now saves you, not as a removal of dirt from the body but as an appeal to God for a good conscience, through the resurrection of Jesus Christ. . ."

For years, churches have used this as a proof text for the essential nature of baptism. We liked to read this and stop at that third comma, "Baptism, which corresponds to this, now saves you." But that isn't what Peter says.

Let's break this down a little bit.

First of all, I've told you about King James and his additions to the Bible. King James was the head of the Anglican church, which was an offshoot of the Catholics created to allow the English king more freedom to do whatever he wanted.

When they were translating the Bible, if King James thought that the translation would hurt the country or the church, he might make some additions. This is one of those.

The word at the beginning of verse 21 is *baptizo*. This is a Greek word that means "to immerse." When the King James version was translated, this word was problematic because the Anglican church sprinkled. They didn't immerse. In fact, they had problems with groups like the Anabaptists who were being disruptive and wanted to immerse instead of just sprinkle.

King James didn't change the word; he just made up one. He Westernized the Greek word by putting English letters in it and making a new word: *baptize*. If we use that word when we sprinkle, then no one knows the difference. When you make up your own word, you can make it mean anything you want it to mean.

As Peter connects baptism to Noah's flood, we see that submerging water is an intricate part of this process. However, it isn't the end. We like it to end with, "Baptism . . . now saves you." If we do that, though, if we put it all on baptism, we steal the power of salvation from Jesus.

When I was interning as a youth minister, we had a young man who wanted to place membership in our congregation. He was a good, godly young man. He was active in Fellowship of Christian Athletes and a leader in his high school. However, our elders would not allow him to place membership unless he was re-baptized. Their argument was that the right words weren't said over him. They were also concerned that his baptism hadn't happened in the right place. They were putting the entire weight of this young man's salvation on the act of baptism.

When Hilary's sister got married, her husband was cornered in their small church in East Texas. He was told to place membership and be re-baptized. I could go on and on with many other examples. We continually find reasons that people must jump through the exact hoop that we place in front of them.

The reasoning for these is that they had to be done "correctly." They had to be done with the right words spoken over them. They had to be done in the correct water.

When we do that, folks, we've gone back to the holy bath water that Jesus has already thrown out!

Peter doesn't stop with "Baptism now saves you." Instead, he says that the power is not in the water, but in the resurrection:

> "Baptism, which corresponds to this, now saves you, not as a removal of dirt from the body but as an appeal to God for a good conscience, through the resurrection of Jesus Christ . . . " (v.21).

Did you catch that? He wrote, "not as the removal of dirt from the body"! There is no power in this water. No holiness. No hocus pocus. This is only an outward sign of submission. The same submission that Peter just got through discussing earlier in chapters 2 and 3.

Now before someone goes off saying, "Jeff is preaching that baptism is not essential." Stop it. That's not what I said. When someone asks me if baptism is essential to salvation, I simply say there is no example of a non-baptized Christian in the New Testament. Can God save you if you haven't been baptized? Well, He wouldn't be much of a God if He couldn't. But I want to be just like Jesus in my life. And if Jesus thought baptism was important enough for Him, why would I think I was any better?

But let's not go bringing back the jars of holy bath water. There is no holiness in the water. There is no magic in the words.

The power of baptism is found in the resurrection of Jesus Christ.

Peter makes that expressly clear here. It isn't about washing. It isn't about me. It's about an appeal to God that can only be made through the power of the resurrection of Jesus Christ.

Remember when we talked about Peter's journey from zero to hero? What was the deciding factor? The resurrection of Jesus. Peter lived it. He witnessed it. And it forever impacted his life.

When he talks here about baptism, he is talking about a spiritual connection of my obedience to the divine obedience demonstrated by Jesus in going to the cross. It is only the power of the resurrection of Jesus that gives any power whatsoever.

Jesus took the idea of holy bath water and replaced it with jars filled with wine.

That wine is what, to us as Christians, reminds us and connects us with His shed blood.

When Jesus instituted the Lord's Supper, He called it the "blood of the covenant." That's because the power is not in the water; it is in the blood.

Don't get so focused on the bath water that you miss the party. Jesus always saves the best for last. He also invites us to His table. To drink His cup. At the feast of the King.

Discussion Questions

1. If you were God come to earth, how would you begin your ministry? With what miracle would you begin?

2. Tell about a time that compares to the wine running out at the wedding of Cana. Maybe a wedding you were involved in or perhaps a party. Have you ever experienced or witnessed something similar?

3. In addition to baptism, are there any other rituals in today's church that we make requirements for salvation? Name some other "holy bath water"-type rituals that we emphasize too much.

4. If you feel comfortable, share with the group your baptism story. How did you feel? How have your thoughts, feelings, and understanding changed since you have been a Christian?

CHAPTER SEVEN

Alien Membership

"Sometimes I think the surest sign that intelligent life exists elsewhere in the universe is that none of it has tried to contact us.
— Bill Watterson

I have a Sam's Club card. It signifies my special status... I am a member. They won't let someone in without one of these. Just try to sneak in without it; they'll jump on you. Oh sure, you can walk around and look, but to truly experience the joys of Sam's Club, you must be a member. Since I pay my membership fee, I expect a certain level of treatment when I go in there. I expect to be able to find things I don't really need in obscenely larger quantities than I'll ever use. I expect to be treated with respect and courtesy when the clerks tell me they don't know what aisle that's on. I expect a certain level of treatment.

I also have a Target Circle Card, 'cause I'm a member. Every time you check out at a Target, they'll ask you if you have one. "Do you have a Circle Card?" If you don't, they look at you as if to say, "You poor, ignorant, clueless sap." Not me! I'm a member. With this little beauty, I can save five whole percent on stuff! If something is too expensive at Sam's, I can drive over to a Target and save five percent! Isn't that great?

I also have a gym membership card. This thing lets me get into a tight little room where I torture myself for at least 45 minutes! I get that privilege because I'm a member. That's right. I pay my dues, and I expect the equipment to be working and accessible so that I can feel better about myself when I go home and eat that pizza later that night!

When I was in high school, I dated a girl from "the other side of the tracks." I was just an old east Texas redneck boy, so I didn't know much about her social circles. One night her father had me out to dinner with the family.

"We'll just go to the club," he said.

That meant *country club*. I was a backwoods boy, and I had never been to a country club before. I mean it was posh. People just waited on him and brought him whatever his heart desired. I asked him about it, and he told me he had access to two swimming pools, a golf course, the clubhouse, and numerous other amenities. I was impressed.

"Wow!" That's pretty awesome!"

He said, "Yeah, I guess membership has its privileges."

Now I'm a member of Elkins Lake Country Club. I have access to two swimming pools, a golf course, a clubhouse, and numerous other amenities. Whenever I need anything, they just ask for my member number. When I go eat, they just want my member number. When I enrolled Allie in tennis camp, they said, "We'll put it on your member number." I guess membership *does* have its privileges.

That's what we've come to understand *membership* to mean. Whether it's a club, or a gym, or a community. Whether it's Costco, AARP, or any other professional organization, we expect certain services and attention from membership.

Alien Membership

We have a culture that strives to find belonging. We want to be included. We want to be a member. We want to be part of something and preferably something exclusive. That consumer membership culture permeates our society. We want priveliges that go along with membership. That also bleeds over into the church.

When I talk to people about church, I'll hear things like:

- What do you offer for children?
- What do you have for teens?
- What kind of women's ministry do you have?
- What do you have for men?
- What does your church offer for families?
- What do you offer for seniors?
- What do you have for singles?• Do you have anything special for married couples?

What are the privileges that come with membership? What do you have to offer me? What is there that should influence me to belong to your group? What are the benefits of membership?

Our consumer culture truly wants to craft church to fit the mold of those old Burger King ads: Have it your way!

Truthfully, isn't that what our churches are all fighting about? Having it our way?

One side wants the church to look just like it did in 1950. The other side wants church to look just like it does on TV. Still another side wants to look just like the megachurch in the city, and another side wants to look like the 20-member church from their childhood.

But the bottom line is this: I want it to be my way. I'm a member. Membership has its privileges.

Is that what Jesus had in mind? Is that the group of those "called out" for whom He died?

This membership mentality doesn't make us into followers of Jesus who live transformed lives as aliens in the world; it makes us fans, consumers of Christian culture. We buy the t-shirts, the CDs, and the books, but is it really changing our lives?

After a while though, we lose the fire. The excitement we once felt about church begins to wane, and we look for membership elsewhere.

Somewhere that will "better meet my needs." Somewhere that will give us what we want and let us have it our way. Somewhere with better membership privileges.

One of the best-known but least lived-out stories of Jesus' life is told in John 13:

> Now before the Feast of the Passover, when Jesus knew that his hour had come to depart out of this world to the Father, having loved his own who were in the world, he loved them to the end. During supper, when the devil had already put it into the heart of Judas Iscariot, Simon's son, to betray him, Jesus, knowing that the Father had given all things into his hands, and that he had come from God and was going back to God, rose from supper. He laid aside his outer garments, and taking a towel, tied it around his waist. Then he poured water into a basin and began to wash the disciples' feet and to wipe them with the towel that was wrapped around him. He came to Simon Peter, who said to him, "Lord, do you wash my feet?" Jesus answered him, "What I am doing you do not understand now, but afterward you will understand." Peter said to him, "You shall never wash my feet." Jesus answered him, "If I do not wash you, you have no share with me." Simon Peter said to him, "Lord, not my feet only but also my hands and my head!" Jesus said to him, "The one who has bathed does not need to wash, except for his feet, but is completely clean. And you are clean, but not every one of you." For he knew who was to betray him; that was why he said, "Not all of you are clean."
>
> When he had washed their feet and put on his outer garments and resumed his place, he said to them, "Do you understand

what I have done to you? You call me Teacher and Lord, and you are right, for so I am. If I then, your Lord and Teacher, have washed your feet, you also ought to wash one another's feet. For I have given you an example, that you also should do just as I have done to you. Truly, truly, I say to you, a servant is not greater than his master, nor is a messenger greater than the one who sent him. If you know these things, blessed are you if you do them (1–17).

Now I humbly submit to you that we must find a way to shut out the world's concept of membership and inject Jesus' membership criteria.

Because that's what being Christ-ones, Christians, is all about . . . being like Jesus.

Think about it, how many of Jesus' miracles were for Him? Think about that. How many times do we see Jesus doing things for Himself? When He was thirsty, He didn't conjure up water . . . He waited for the Samaritan woman.

When He was hungry . . . He didn't miraculously make bread appear; He waited for it to be brought. We never read of His healing Himself or caring for Himself. He was always taking food to others, taking water to them, offering healing to them, giving life . . . to them. Always, it's about others.

As followers of Christ, as aliens in this strange world, are we following Jesus in service? Are we picking up the bowl and the towel and ministering to others in our community?

In the Old Testament, priests performed and received ceremonial foot washings before they entered the temple for worship. Foot washing was a serious matter: A basin for foot washing would have been placed between the Tent of Meeting and the altar, so Aaron and his sons could wash before entering the Tent of Meeting, "Whenever they enter the tent of meeting, they shall wash with water so that they will not die" (Exodus 30:20, NIV).

Disregarding the ritual cleansing meant death to a priest.

In John 13:4–5, Jesus "got up from the meal, took off his outer clothing, and wrapped a towel around his waist. After that, he poured water into a basin and began to wash his disciples' feet, drying them with the towel that was wrapped around him."

Jesus has placed the basin between the disciples and the altar, His cross. Through His death and His resurrection, Jesus makes holy all who come to the cross through the power of the Holy Spirit. Through Christ's atoning work on the cross, the disciples and all believers are made holy and righteous before God and then set apart for service in His body, the Church, a holy priesthood of believers. Jesus washes His disciples' feet to purify and cleanse them for their service to God: "Unless I wash you, you have no part with me" (John 13:8).

Jesus anoints the disciples for their new role as priests in the new temple that God will raise up. Jesus ordains them, so they can serve His church when He leaves this world to return to the Father. Through the act of purification, Jesus imparts His holiness to the disciples, so they will be set apart from the world even though they will remain in the world. Jesus teaches His disciples that His holiness, salvation, and purity will all come through Him and His suffering.

Through this simple act of foot washing, Jesus demonstrates to His disciples His eternal role as God's High Priest and Mediator and their part in the priesthood. Even though He must suffer and die, the disciples can by faith be certain that He will never leave them or forsake them.

Scripture says, "During the days of Jesus' life on earth, he offered up prayers and petitions with fervent cries and tears to the one who could save him from death, and he was heard because of his reverent submission.

Son, though he was, he learned obedience from what he suffered and, once made perfect, he became the source of eternal salvation for all who obey him and was designated by God to be high priest in the order of Melchizedek" (Hebrews 5:7–10, NIV).

He is the High Priest of heaven, and through the foot washing, He has ordained His disciples to be priests of the church in the world, He will offer up prayers on their behalf, "he always lives to intercede for them" (Hebrews 7:25) and will empower them through the Holy Spirit to perform their priestly duties to the glory of God.

The church grows, as sinners saved by grace are drawn by the Spirit to the holy altar. As that sinner draws near, she is made pure through the cleansing power of the blood of the Lamb. In submission, that sinner will be baptized and raised a new creature. A new creation, cleansed of the sin that separates and filled with the life-giving power of the Holy Spirit.

Just as the ancient priests would immerse themselves in the Mikvah baptism to cleanse themselves to enter the presence of God, these sinners, now washed and cleansed, become the kingdom of priests that God promised Moses in Exodus 19. These disciples are now priests who remove the soiled clothing of their previous life and receive new garments through the sacrifice of Jesus.

These are the garments they are to make: a breastpiece, an ephod, a robe, a woven tunic, a turban and a sash. They are to make these sacred garments for your brother Aaron and his sons, so they may serve me as priests (Exodus 28:4).

The kingdom of priests are no longer clothed in ephods and turbans but now are outfitted with the "full armor of God" (Ephesians 6:14–17). As Paul writes in 1 Corinthians 15, these priestly disciples have put on the imperishable, and the mortal has put on immortality (1 Corinthians 15:54). These priestly garments are being worn every time the church displays the risen body of Christ to a lost and dying world, when the church offers sacrifices of praise and thanksgiving, when the church is ministering to those who are hurting and lost, whenever the hands and feet of Christ are being demonstrated through the body of the church the blood-bought disciples are wearing their priestly vestments — until the day when we will once again be given new garments. On that day, the church will be given the holy garments of their faith. Robes made white by the sacred blood of Christ. Revelation 7:14 ". . . they have washed their robes and made them white in the blood of the Lamb."

These church members are not country club dues-payers. These members are holy priests of Christ who come together in worship and praise in anticipation of the great congregation of victory when all are gathered together with the resurrected Lord.

"But you are a chosen race, a royal priesthood, a holy nation, a people for his own possession, that you may proclaim the excellencies of him who called you out of darkness into his marvelous light" (1 Peter 2:9–10).

Love, hospitality, and service. Those are the membership privileges given to Christians.

When we say "member," we will mean something totally different, totally alien, than what the world means. Peter says that aliens in this crazy world are going to be about those same three things: love, hospitality, and service.

> The end of all things is at hand; therefore be self-controlled and sober- minded for the sake of your prayers. Above all, keep loving one another earnestly, since love covers a multitude of sins. Show hospitality to one another without grumbling. As each has received a gift, use it to serve one another, as good stewards of God's varied grace: whoever speaks, as one who speaks oracles of God; whoever serves, as one who serves by the strength that God supplies — in order that in everything God may be glorified through Jesus Christ. To him belong glory and dominion forever and ever. Amen (1 Peter 4:7-11).

Above all is love. It's primary. It's first. Even Paul affirms this in 1 Corinthians 13 when he says that love is the greatest. Even greater than hope. Even greater than faith. Love is above all.

Love also covers a multitude of sins. So don't stop. Keep on loving one another.

Do that through your hospitality. That word is *philoxenos* a combination of *philos* (love) and *xenos* (strangers), so literally, it's a lover of strangers. Its only other usage has to do with elders. Elders are to be lovers of strangers. So, when you get the whole, "That guy invites the whole church to his house." That doesn't really qualify you because it isn't what the word is saying, it's looking for the person who is generous and eager to reach out to outsiders and strangers. So again, there's that outward focus that we've been seeing throughout 1 Peter.

And finally service. "As each has received a gift, use it to serve one another, as good stewards of God's varied grace" (v. 10).

Peter, the same as Paul in Ephesians, seems to imply that whatever gifts we have were bestowed on us for two purposes: serving one another and glorifying God.

What's your gift? With what has God blessed you? Generosity? Hospitality? Speaking? Teaching? Whatever your gift, that gift is from God. Your stewardship of that plan involves using that gift to serve others and to glorify God.

So how are you serving? If we look around, we have myriad opportunities to serve. Whether it's buying a 12-pack of sodas for VBS, teaching a Sunday school class, helping with maintenance, singing on the praise team, giving to facilitate ministry, praying, encouragement, the list can go on and on.

That gift is given to you by the grace of God. That's the definition of a gift, you don't earn it. You don't deserve it. It's a gift. That gift is freely given from God.

Peter says stewardship of that grace involves using that gift in service. Paul will say that each has been gifted "to equip the saints for the work of ministry, for building up the body of Christ" (Ephesians 4:12).

So what are our membership rewards? What are our privileges? What does our church have to offer?

We offer a bowl and a towel . . . and a beautiful invitation to join our Lord in service as a priesthood of believers.

So are you ready to join this alienated group? Are you ready to envision church in a different way?

Instead of asking what church can offer me, we want to return to the call of Jesus . . . a call not to membership but to service. To serve the body, to build up the body, to reach out to those who are lost.

A mission that involves growing together in faith, bringing hope to a dying world but above all . . . to be known as a group of people that loves, that loves with actions instead of mere words.

That's church mission. That's what vision of living in an alienated nation looks like. I humbly encourage you to catch that vision. Be a card-carrying member . . . of Christ.

Discussion Questions

1. What memberships do you have? Do you have any with you? Share your memberships with the group.

2. Jeff says that we expect certain privileges with membership. Is that true in the church? How have you seen that "membership mentality" play out?

3. Have you ever thought of yourself as a priest (or priestess)? How does seeing ourselves as priests change the way we relate to God? To one another? To the world?

Alien Membership

4. What are your gifts? If you can't think of any, ask someone close to you — a significant other, parent, friend — who can share with you, in love, how they see your gifts at work.
5. How can you use your gifts in hospitality and service?

CHAPTER EIGHT

Alien Trials

"Some people don't believe in aliens. I do believe in aliens. But I believe they gave up on people a long time ago. Wouldn't you? I think there's a few liberal aliens out there, still hanging in."
— Joe Rogan

"I can't find a heartbeat," the doctor said as he looked at the sonogram. It was just five little words. Five little words that hit me like a kick in the stomach. I didn't know whether to cry, pray, or scream. The truth? I really felt like punching something. My wife and I walked out, holding each other, but with little other communication. What do you say? I had to do the male thing of "being strong." You know, that typical male reaction that has been bred into us through years of male bonding and hours of John Wayne. Be strong. Be stoic. Be silent. Be brave. The truth was I felt anything but strong. My stomach was in my throat, and I couldn't tell if I was about to lose my lunch or just crumble right there in the parking lot. But I had to be strong.

ALIENATED

It didn't really work out well. For me, being strong became being silent. In a moment when my wife dearly needed my comfort or emotional support, I withdrew into myself and put up a wall of stoicism around me. Though I called it being strong, it was really more like hiding. I walked around for the next few days in a bit of a haze. My work suffered. My home life suffered. I was so out of it that when I took my wife to the movies to get our minds somewhere else, I left the car parked on the curb in front of the theater box office. Not in a parking place. Not in a garage. Right there in the pull-through drop off area . . . for the entire movie! When we finally came out, (I can't even remember what movie we saw), I couldn't remember where we had parked. I was totally somewhere else — wrapped up in my own combination of self-pity, despair, and a false sense of machismo that wouldn't let me show any of it.

I come from a spiritual background. I grew up in church my entire life, and after a few years of searching in my teens, I attended a Bible university and earned a bachelor's degree in Bible. I spent six years in youth ministry before being called into teaching, and I finally ended up in the pulpit. I felt that I had a solid spiritual foundation that prepared me to weather any storm. I was wrong. The storm came, and I was totally unprepared for aftermath that lay ahead. The physical storm (Hurricane Rita) hit the next week. I spent the few days beforehand preparing, secretly thankful to have something to focus on other than the loss of my child. I nailed boards to windows, stockpiled food and water, and distributed candles and flashlights through our home. I drove past the freeways jam-packed with people running from the storm and felt a unique kinship with the situation. I felt the same way in my heart. There was a huge storm enveloping my life, and I would have given anything to be able to run away. To be an evacuee from the destruction that this emotional and spiritual hurricane was wreaking in my heart. Finally, as the storm moved away to the east of us, I stood alone in the street outside my house. The wind whipped through, and the light rain pelted my face. As I stood there, the tears finally began to flow, and I asked the question that had been in my heart, but my mouth had been too afraid to utter, "Why?"

Why would a God of love allow this to happen? Why would a loving God take my baby? What had I done? What debt did I owe? As I faced the black, billowing clouds and the darkness of a night without electricity, I looked to the heavens and begged, "Why?" That was my first step. Sounds simple and even a bit too simplistic, but that is where I started. I believe that from that point, God began to answer that question in my life.

That quest, that search, that question is commonly referred to in "preacher talk" as "theodicy." Roughly, this means the question of suffering. Why does an all-powerful God not use that power to alleviate suffering in the world?

Why does an all-knowing God seem to not notice when I am suffering? Why does a God of love allow His beloved children to suffer and hurt? These questions plague believers and seekers alike. There are many who identify these questions, or questions like them, as their key barriers to faith.

The problem of suffering so plagues Christianity that it has become something that no one talks about. Churches today are so busy giving sermons on "How to Live Your Best Life Now" and "Claiming God's Blessings in Your Life" that it's seen as almost a lack of faith to talk about struggle, doubt, or suffering. But those things are real. That's where most of us live.

A few years ago, Jan Crouch, one of the founders of TBN and a longtime televangelist, passed away. As the light of publicity shown on her life's work, people couldn't help but question how a woman who reportedly had enough faith to raise a chicken from the dead could herself succumb to a sudden stroke. A woman who reportedly prophesied various events in our world could not see her own demise. This is the problem many in the world have with Christianity today. They see a faith portrayed as fake or worse, naïve, to the real problems of the world. They see a people who are morally self-righteous, superior, and condescending to others around them. They also look at us and ask the same question: "Where is God when we are suffering?"

Why do bad things happen to good people?

That isn't really something for which I'm seeking an answer, it's more rhetorical.

The great question: Why do we suffer? Why is there pain or suffering in our world? Why can you seem to be doing everything right and only meet with heartache and pain?

There have been lots of attempts to answer this question, but if we're honest, they all seem to fall a little flat.

Go back as far as you can go, and this question has been addressed. Go all the way back to Job.

Though it isn't the first book in the table of contents, Job is the oldest book in the Bible. It might be the oldest book in the world. It's older than Genesis, though Genesis covers older material. An analogy would be if I now wrote a book about JFK and compared it to a book written 10 years ago about Reagan. The Reagan book is older than my book, but mine covers earlier material. Genesis covers creation to the flood, and then the era of the patriarchs. Job is set in the era of the patriarchs, but is, in fact, an older book than Genesis.

We know this because of the age of the Hebrew used. Languages evolve through time. Compare modern English to "The Tell-Tale Heart" by Edgar Allan Poe, from 1843, which uses phrases like, "You fancy me mad." Today we'd say, "You think I'm crazy." Even further back, say, 1611, we read English like this: "And he said, Draw not nigh hither: put off thy shoes from off thy feet, for the place whereon thou standest is holy ground" (Exodus 3:5, KJV). The difference in 1611, and now is over 400 years, and today we'd read, "'Do not come closer,' He said. 'Remove the sandals from your feet, for the place where you are standing is holy ground'" (CSB). That's only 400 years difference; the Hebrew Bible covers Hebrew written from about 1800 BC to at least 430 BC, maybe later. That's over 1,200 years of change! Linguists can judge the age of a document based on how old its diction is.

The oldest Hebrew: Job. The Hebrew in Job is so old, it's unique. It's actually often called "Paleo-Hebrew." Job was written in the time of the Patriarchs.

Genesis was written, or compiled, by Moses, some 430+ years later!

Addressing the problem of theodicy — the vindication of the justice of God in the light of humanity's suffering — Job is a rich theological work setting out a variety of perspectives. It has been widely and often extravagantly praised for its literary qualities, with Alfred, Lord Tennyson calling it "the greatest poem, whether of ancient or modern literature."

Because of a reference in James, we have come to believe that Job is about patience. However, if you actually read all of Job, you'll find that this is not the case. It isn't about the patience of Job.

It's more about God. Is God good? Is God just? And how would He have us react to the suffering that we would face in our world?

Job gives us a glimpse into the backstage area of the cosmos, but it really doesn't tackle the question of why we suffer. Suffering seems to be a given.

There's the great cosmic bet — the bet between God and Satan. The book gives us a glimpse into heaven, and, in that glimpse, we see Satan before the throne of God. God asks, "Where have you been? What have you been up to?" Satan replies that he's been wandering about the earth. So begin the trials of Job.

That's the way I've heard this book referenced my entire life: "the trials of Job." For a kid raised in the television age, that conjures up some interesting pictures. I grew up with a mom who loved "Ironsides" and "Perry Mason." I watched lots of trials in my youth. When I hear "trials," I think of "Matlock" or "The People's Court." In my life I have seen the Gotti trials, the O.J. Simpson trial, and the Enron trial. So when I hear about the trials of Job, I picture God sitting as judge over a courtroom where poor Job must prove his faith.

This is what I was always taught about the story of Job. I was taught that Job's faith was tested. Having grown up in the Texas school systems, I know about tests. We were continually being bombarded with the latest standardized testing designed to determine if we were actually learning anything in our classes. So when I thought of Job's faith being tested, I thought I understood what that meant. As a young man growing up in the church, I learned all about the patience of Job. That's what was continually emphasized to us: the patience of Job.

In the story, Job's faith is tested. First, Satan attacks his possessions. He destroys everything that Job owns or holds dear in the material world, including his children. He does this because he is sure that Job will curse God for his losses. Yet, that doesn't happen. So Satan again appears before God and asks permission to strike Job in his body. He asks permission to strike him with illness because surely then he will curse God and die. But Satan doesn't stop there. He attacks with the words of those around him.

Job's wife is one who continually says, "I don't understand how you can cling to faith while God allows your whole world to be destroyed. Curse God and die!"

As if that weren't enough, then his friends arrive. They give Job the same faulty theology we talked about in the last chapter. They tell Job that surely he has sinned in some truly heinous way for God to be this angry with him. "Such is the fate God allots the wicked, the heritage appointed for them by God" (Job 20:29, NIV). All this is orchestrated to get Job to break, yet Job's faith remains steadfast.

Alien Trials

This is where the story usually stopped in Sunday school. We were told that when hard times come, we should be patient and continue to praise God just as Job did. that isn't the whole story though. There are a few things that we need to learn from this story other than "be patient and suffer in silence." The first of which is that God is a "big boy." Somehow we've gotten it into our heads that God is fragile. We believe that He, like many of our brethren, will be cringing at our words or will be easily offended and hurt. God is a "big boy." If you learn nothing else from Job, learn that God is big enough to hear our complaints. I had always been taught that Job simply suffered in silence and trusted that God knew what He was doing. That is not the case.

Listen to some of Job's words:

> "I cry out to you, God, but you do not answer; I stand up, but you merely look at me. You turn on me ruthlessly; with the might of your hand you attack me" (Job 30:20-21, NIV).

> "If only I knew where to find him; if only I could go to his dwelling! I would state my case before him and fill my mouth with arguments. I would find out what he would answer me," (Job 23:3-5).

Job doesn't lose faith. He does not curse God, nor does he simply suffer in silence. He cries out. He asks "God, why have you turned your back on me? What have I done to make you attack me?" He asks for an appearance. He asks for a trial so that God will answer his arguments. "What do you have to say for yourself?" When I think of this, I think of the scene in Forrest Gump where Lt. Dan rides out the storm strapped to the mast of the ship as he attacks God. Job didn't curse God. He didn't attack God. But he did ask why.

If you are like me, now you want to know why. Why me? Why my baby? But somehow, we are conditioned to believe that God cannot handle such direct questioning. That's why I say this is an important lesson. God is a "big boy." He can handle it. You are not going to offend Him, or hurt His feelings, or make Him turn away because you ask why. Anger is still an act of faith.

You don't get angry with Bigfoot or with ghosts or anything you don't actually believe in. Anger is an act of faith, so don't fear. This is part of growing in a relationship.

The flipside of that coin is, however, not to expect any revelations or answers. In the book of Job, God finally does address him, just as Job has been requesting. He answers the things Job has laid on Him. How does He answer it?

> "Where were you when I laid the earth's foundation? Tell me, if you understand, Who marked off its dimensions? Surely you know! Who stretched a measuring line across it? On what were its footings set, or who laid its cornerstone — while the morning stars sang together and all the angels shouted for joy?" (Job 38:4-7, NIV).

And He doesn't let up. God goes on to ask if Job has entered the storehouses of snow or found the place where lightning is dispersed. He asks who fathers the rain and what womb produces ice? He asks about the stars in the heavens. He asks about the lions, the ravens, the mountain goats, the ostrich, and the horse. God says if you know so much that you can question Me, then answer these simple questions. When you can tell me where the sun comes from, then I'll tell you what you want to know. God basically says, "Why don't you let me be God, because I don't think you are qualified for the job." So, don't expect any instant answers. Don't expect God to say, "Oh, I'm sorry. Let me show you my reasoning on this one." No. If anything, God laughs that we have any grounds to question anything. But He still cares. That is the other big lesson of Job. God cares. God sees. He takes notice.

So why do bad things happen? Why do we suffer?

The same theology of Job's friends continues to be taught. Fast forward to the New Testament; they are still wrestling with this question. They are still residing in the same theological framework of Deuteronomic Theology in which Job's friends were living. Obedience = blessing. Disobedience = curse.

This just isn't biblical. You'll, no doubt, hear a lot of folks talk about karma as the spiritual framework of Buddhism has infiltrated our culture. It's the same idea. Good works = blessings. Bad deeds = curses.

Even Jesus' disciples wrestled with this idea. They even brought it up to Him.

You find that exchange in John 9. Jesus and the disciples are walking along as He teaches and preaches. He has just had a run-in with an angry group of Jews who were ready to stone Him because He claimed to be God. As they walk along, they come upon a beggar beside the road. A man, the Bible tells us, who had been blind from birth. The disciples ask, "Who sinned, this man or his parents, that he was born blind?" (John 9:2, NIV).

If I'm honest, that's been my question. When we had our miscarriage, I stood in the middle of a rainstorm as a hurricane was blowing in and shouted that very question at God. *WHY? What did I do to deserve this?*

Jesus' answer in John 9 stumped me at first.

"'Neither this man nor his parents sinned,' said Jesus, 'but this happened so that the works of God might be displayed in him" (John 9:3).

And I thought, *So what?* I mean, Jesus was saying that this man was blind so that Jesus could heal him. It had nothing to do with me. This man was born blind so that the work of God could be displayed in his life. Surely, I had to keep searching. This didn't apply to me. Or did it? If you read on you'll see Jesus talk about this again in John 11, the story of Lazarus. In that story, Jesus told His disciples, "Lazarus

ALIENATED

is dead, and for your sake I am glad I was not there, so that you may believe." Later he told Martha, "Did I not tell you that if you believed, you will see the glory of God?" (14–15, 40).

In his wonderful book, *The Problem of Pain*, C.S. Lewis writes, "We can rest contentedly in our sins and in our stupidities, and everyone who has watched gluttons shoveling down the most exquisite foods as if they did not know what they were eating, will admit that we can ignore even pleasure. But pain insists upon being attended to. God whispers to us in our pleasures, speaks in our consciences, but shouts in our pain: it is His megaphone to rouse a deaf world."

I had been asking "why," but what I had really wanted to know was "why me?" I knew that I probably shouldn't be asking that question. I knew that it made me sound pitiful and helpless, but truthfully, that is what was in my heart. Why me? Why did this have to happen to my baby? Why did this have to happen to my family? What did I do to deserve this? Yet, that isn't the question the disciples ask Jesus here. What did this guy, or his family, do to deserve this kind of pain in his life?

"This happened so that the work of God might be displayed in his life." Could that be the real message? That all this had happened so that the work of God might be displayed in my life? C.S. Lewis said that God shouts in our pain. Is God shouting at me now? I began to meditate on this. What if the whole purpose of this had been for God to find a way to shout into my life?

Am I being arrogant?

As I continued to search and to look for the answer, I found another quote that merits sharing:

> "In all fairness, if we ask the 'Why me?' question in regard to our burdens, we should also ask it in regard to our blessings.

Alien Trials

> "We take for granted 100 days of perfect health, and then grumble about one day of aches and pains.
>
> "We drive the freeway hundreds of times without incident, and then ask, 'Why me?' the one time we have a flat tire or engine trouble.
>
> "We casually accept the fact when our family is together for the holidays, but when we are separated, we dwell on our loneliness.
>
> "How often do we say, 'Why me?' as we count our blessings?
>
> "Rather than feeling sad about what we don't have, doesn't it make more sense to feel a kind of rollicking rejoicing over everything we do have?"
>
> — Dr. Dale Turner, MSC Health Action News, Vol. XVII, No. 11, Nov./Dec., 1997, p. 1

Maybe I had been asking the wrong question. Why me? Why not me? For years, I had been the one who was the voice of reason. I had stood by as people asked these very questions. I had been the one who laid out the clichéd platitudes and felt smug and spiritual about myself. But did God promise me that I would have a life without pain? Did God promise me that there would be no hurting? No.

Peter is not a prosperity preacher. He makes no claims of fantastic blessings or supernatural wealth. Instead he tells his those who were alienated repeatedly throughout the book that suffering is coming. Suffering is coming. Don't be surprised when it hits you.

> Beloved, do not be surprised at the fiery trial when it comes upon you to test you, as though something strange were happening to you. But rejoice insofar as you share Christ's sufferings, that you may also rejoice and be glad when his glory is revealed. If

> you are insulted for the name of Christ, you are blessed, because the Spirit of glory and of God rests upon you. But let none of you suffer as a murderer or a thief or an evildoer or as a meddler. Yet if anyone suffers as a Christian, let him not be ashamed, but let him glorify God in that name. For it is time for judgment to begin at the household of God; and if it begins with us, what will be the outcome for those who do not obey the gospel of God? And "If the righteous is scarcely saved, what will become of the ungodly and the sinner?" (1 Peter 4:12-18).

Peter says, "Don't be surprised when the fiery trial comes upon you." It's easy for us to look at that and go, "Huh?" What fiery trial? To understand this, we have to go further back into the book.

> "In this you rejoice, though now for a little while, if necessary, you have been grieved by various trials, so that the tested genuineness of your faith — more precious than gold that perishes though it is tested by fire — may be found to result in praise and glory and honor at the revelation of Jesus Christ." (1 Peter 1:6-7).

There's that concept again. Trials. Now, again, we aren't talking about Perry Mason and Matlock. So, this is not all about accusation and proving my worth. The words he uses here have to do with refining. Specifically, they are used when talking about refining gold.

Refining with flame is one of the oldest methods of refining metals. Mentioned even in the Bible, refining by fire is the preferable method for larger quantities of gold. In ancient times, this form of refining involved a craftsman sitting next to a hot fire with molten gold being stirred and skimmed in a crucible to remove the impurities or dross that rose to the top of the molten metal. With flames reaching temperatures in excess of 1000° C, this job was definitely a dangerous occupation for the gold refiner. The tradition remains largely untouched today with the exception of a few advancements in safety and precision.

So when Peter is talking about "fiery trials," he is talking about a process that leads to purification, process the removes the impurities and increases the value and worth of the object. A refiner's fire.

He says that our trials today are upon us to refine us. These trials that we suffer today are for the purification of our faith. Our faith is being removed of impurities. Our faith is being molded and cleansed into something even more valuable than it was before.

Suffering is that refiner's fire. It molds us. It changes us. We are who we are, not because of the manifold blessings and prosperity that God has heaped upon us, but because we have learned to trust Him through the fire.

Even psychology is catching up to this concept.

Carl Jung, the great psychologist, once said, "Neurosis is always a substitute for legitimate suffering."

What we'd like to do is avoid all suffering and pain. We'd like to avoid the shame of the confession, the entry into rehab or therapy, the request for help, the grief of loss, the effects of consequences that are rightly coming our way, the sting of disappointment in the face of failure, the hurt in a faltering relationship.

To avoid the pain, we develop neurotic coping mechanisms. We self-medicate. We blame. We distract ourselves. We avoid. We pretend.

We avoid legitimate suffering by burying it under neurotic symptoms. Rather than suffering directly we suffer indirectly through symptoms of neurotic avoidance. So how would you congeal Peter's advice?

Life is going to hurt at times, and when it begins to hurt, don't panic. Don't be surprised that this is happening to you.

ALIENATED

If you panic and try to avoid the hurt, you will often bring more pain into your life than the actual hurt. Don't over-correct in your panic to avoid the pain, or you'll drive off the road and crash.

Don't run away from, avoid, deny, repress, mask, or medicate your hurt. Just let it hurt.

Let the hurt wash over you like a wave, and let it pass.

If you fight it, if you try to avoid the hurt, you'll stop living.

You'll stop being fully present in the moment, always insulating and protectively distancing yourself.

That, or you'll become frozen in time by hurt you are unwilling to face or feel.

You'll start becoming a bundle of neurotic symptoms used to protect yourself from the pain and risk of living.

So learn to suffer well. How do we suffer well? We trust. We serve. That's the key. Look at the end of 1 Peter 4:

> "Therefore let those who suffer according to God's will entrust their souls to a faithful Creator while doing good" (1 Peter 4:19).

Trust that God is in control. Trust that the Shepherd is leading His sheep where they need to go. Trust Him.

And stop focusing on your suffering. Stop focusing on yourself. Do good.

Get busy about kingdom business. Not worrying about "why me," but developing an attitude of "why NOT me?"

If my Lord and Savior would suffer, why NOT me?

So I will trust God, and I will walk with Him in service.

Learn to suffer well. Because regardless of where you are currently, you either have endured or will endure suffering. That suffering can be a refining that purifies, magnifies, and increases your faith.

Discussion Questions

1. What suffering have you experienced in your life? Have you ever asked God, "Why?"

2. Jeff says, "Anger is an act of faith." How do you think that is true?

3. How can we help those engrossed in suffering find ways to entrust their souls while doing good?

4. How can our churches better reach out to those suffering, hurting, grieving or needing that support?

CHAPTER NINE

Alien Leaders

"Sometimes I wish the aliens would abduct me and crown me as their leader."
— George Noory

I'll never forget when my Uncle Otis died. He was my grandmother's brother, and she loved him dearly. They took vacations together, and he and his family either visited us or had us come to their home in Beaumont throughout my childhood. He and my grandmother loved each other, and it broke her heart when he passed away.

We were all together in my grandparent's home when some people from church stopped by to check on her. One of them, an elder in the church, began talking about my uncle, who had also been an elder in a church near his home in Beaumont. He actually died in an elder's meeting (now I've thought that was going to happen before to me, but it actually did happen to him).

This elder in our local church proceeded to talk about how "liberal" that church down there was. It seems that during a big storm, the church had participated with other denominations in taking care of the needs of people displaced by flooding, and he hoped that cooperation didn't "tarnish Otis's crown" now that he had gone on to judgment.

I wanted to punch him in the mouth.

He went on to talk about how there was only one true church, and it shouldn't associate with anyone else. He talked about command, example and necessary inference. He talked about "speaking where the Bible speaks and being silent where the Bible is silent." He rambled on in judgment and condescension, talking about a church he had never attended and making passive aggressive judgments toward a man he had never met.

I wanted to punch him in the mouth.

There was a smug arrogance in that entire exchange. He was pleased to hear himself and felt that we should all be as well. Forget that he had no idea what he was talking about and every single theological and biblical thought he espoused in that entire lecture was wrong. He was an elder.

Later, I asked my grandfather why he didn't punch him in the mouth, because this man's words were obviously hurting my grandmother. My grandfather said that the Bible says we should respect our elders, and he guessed that even meant when they weren't being respectful themselves.

That picture has stayed with me. In fact, I've heard many similar stories. I've heard of elders who glory in their position, I've heard of preachers who expect special treatment, I've heard of a large number of church leaders who abuse their position, expecting the world around them to like it.

Now before you sit back and say, "Boy, Jeff really gave it to those elders," I think a lot of this is our fault. Yours and mine. As members of churches, we are responsible for a lot of this problem. I think there are a lot of us preachers who are responsible for this problem.

Alien Leaders

The way my church chose elders when I was growing up was through a caucus — a political process. Every time it came up, you knew who was "running for office." They were shaking hands and kissing babies. They were working the crowd because they were trying to build up a constituency.

Elder selection was one of the most divisive things I saw growing up, because everyone divided into their special interest groups and chose "their man." That guy was taking their agenda, and he was going to be their representative at the elders' table.

It's definitely one of the most unscriptural notions I've ever heard.

When elder selection time came, certain passages were always dusted off and preached. We would hear lots of lessons about "qualifications" of elders. We would hear about being the "husband of one wife." We heard a lot about that one! We would hear about being of "sound doctrine." (That one was usually code that meant this person believed what I believed). We would hear a lot about "godly children" and "ruling their household." Through it all, we ended up getting men "elected" who met a pre-conceived checklist and would represent a particular agenda.

That's why this problem is our fault.

One of the passages you didn't hear about a lot in elder selection is our text. As Peter is wrapping up his letter to the "aliens" he has been teaching, he takes a moment to speak to their leaders. Listen to what he has to say:

> So I exhort the elders among you, as a fellow elder and a witness of the sufferings of Christ, as well as a partaker in the glory that is going to be revealed: shepherd the flock of God that is among you, exercising oversight, not under compulsion, but willingly, as God would have you; not for shameful gain, but eagerly; not domineering over those in your charge, but being examples to the flock. And when the chief Shepherd appears, you will receive

> the unfading crown of glory. Likewise, you who are younger, be subject to the elders. Clothe yourselves, all of you, with humility toward one another, for "God opposes the proud but gives grace to the humble" (1 Peter 5:1-5).

When I read these verses, I cannot help but laugh a little. I mean, we have to remember who is writing these words. These deep thoughts on leadership flow from the reckless, headstrong, and obstinate apostle who was always the first to arrive but also the first to run away. There is also a strong sense that Peter is a changed man whose view of leadership has been radically transformed. Peter's perspective on leadership is now that of Jesus. In these verses addressed primarily to elders, we see a clear link to the teaching of Jesus in the Gospels, a teaching Peter came to embrace for himself and now is teaching others.

The existence of elders as spiritual leaders goes back to Israel's Old Testament times when 70 elders were appointed and divinely empowered to assist Moses in leading the people of God (see Numbers 11:16–30). They persisted throughout Israel's history (see Deuteronomy 25:7; 1 Kings 20:8; 21:11; 2 Kings 6:32; Ezra 10:8) and into New Testament times, where they are mentioned in conjunction with the chief priests, scribes, and Pharisees (see Matthew 16:21; 21:23; 26:3, 57; 27:1, 3; Acts 4:5; 6:12; 24:1).

Elders also played a role in secular rule as well.

Elders emerged as the highest human authority in the New Testament church, assisted by deacons (see Philippians 1:1; 1 Timothy 3:1–13; Titus 1:5–9; James 5:14). Elders of the church first appear in Acts 11:30, where the monies collected for the poor in Judea were sent to the elders. In Acts 14:23, we are told that Paul and Barnabas appointed elders in the churches founded on their first missionary journey. In Acts 15, the apostles and elders of the church met in

Jerusalem at what became known as the Jerusalem Council to clarify the gospel as it related to Gentile converts. Throughout the New Testament, the church is ruled by a plurality of elders with no central "head" of the church other than her Lord Jesus Christ. When Peter addresses the elders in our text, he is addressing those who have been divinely appointed and entrusted with the spiritual leadership of the church.

When Peter exhorts elders to "shepherd the flock" (1 Peter 5:2), we are reminded of Jesus' words to Peter in John 21:15–17. When Peter instructs church leaders not to "lord it over" those under their care (1 Peter 5:3), we are reminded of our Lord's words in Matthew 20:25–28. When Peter urges all his readers to "clothe yourselves with humility," we can hardly miss the reference here to the example and teaching of Jesus in John 13 when He clothed Himself with a towel as a servant and washed the disciples' feet.

Peter is a changed man from the Peter of the Gospels. His teaching is vastly different from what we would have expected of him from the Gospel accounts. His teaching is also different from much that is taught about leadership today, even in Christian circles.

Peter's words are not just to elders nor even to leaders. These are words addressed to all. We should all listen carefully, looking to the Holy Spirit to make their meaning and application clear in our minds — and also in our lives.

Peter addresses a lot of our ideas about church leadership right here. In this brief section, we learn a lot about what it means to lead in church.

First, it's plural. The words used here to address church leaders are always plural. There are always multiples. That's why a lot of churches today are moving away from a single minister leadership model. As people study the text, they are realizing that a plurality of elders is the biblical model.

Peter uses three of the big words used today to talk about leaders. Each of these gives a different facet of what these people are to look like.

He uses *presbuteros*, which is translated *elders* or *presbyters*, referring to someone who is wise and advanced in years. They have life experience. They are not young and impetuous. Part of being an elder involves being a bit elderly. Now I know that isn't popular today. We have lots of younger men who are stepping into leadership, and I'm not saying that these men are not qualified. I am saying that this word generally is used to refer to people who have some wisdom and some life under their belt.

He uses *poimen*, which is translated *shepherd* or *pastor*. Shepherding here is a verb. It's an action. Shepherd the flock of God that is among you. He doesn't say this is your church. It's God's flock. Rarely was the shepherd the owner of the sheep, yet it was his job to make sure they were safe and well cared for. It was his job to be responsible for feeding them, caring for them, for their safety and security, and for bringing them back if they wandered away. That's important. If you aspire to be a shepherd one day, I'm gonna tell you (and our current shepherds will back me up on this) only about 10% of that job takes place in that conference room. You can't shepherd sheep from a conference room. You have to be among them. You have to be involved with them. You have to participate in their lives.

Shepherds lived with the sheep. They ate with them, slept among them, walked with them, and were involved in their lives.

Now don't get me wrong. This is not a democracy. The sheep don't get to set the agenda. If you're hoping to select "your man," you're still wrong. Chris Seidman said, "Shepherds don't wait for sheep to tell them when it's time to move pastures." Shepherding is about leading. It's about moving the sheep when they don't want to be moved. It's about doing things that sheep find offensive or uncomfortable because it's the best thing for the sheep. That's leadership.

Peter also uses the word, *episkopos*, which is translated *overseer* or *bishop*. This word was always used in the ancient world to refer to a manager or someone who was in charge of something. Overseeing doesn't involve being an overlord.

Peter says oversight in the church doesn't come in the form of executive orders, it comes in the form of leading by example. That means stepping out in places you may be uncomfortable. It means having the hard conversations. It means making the tough decisions. It means that this task is no picnic.

Peter wraps it all up with a simple word that often gets left off those elder qualification checklists: Humility.

> Clothe yourselves, all of you, with humility toward one another,
> for "God opposes the proud but gives grace to the humble"
> (1 Peter 5:5).

The literal translation of that passage reads this way:

> And all being subject to one another, put on humility, because
> God sets Himself against the proud but offers His grace to
> the humble.

This is not just about leaders. This is not about a political office. This is not about hierarchy.

This is about submission. Earlier in this book, Peter talked about submission to authority, submission in the homes and submission in the workplace; now he comes full circle and says the church should be the model of that. As we subject ourselves to one another.

See, that's the key. Peter knows that's the key.

You can't abuse another human being, you can't injure another human being, you can't beat down another human being if you are subject to them.

How much different would our world be if we lived by this principle? Ghandi supposedly once said that he thought Christianity was a great idea, it's just too bad no one had ever tried it.

But even moreso, God is saying that if you continue to bicker and fight while holding on to the pride of your right doctrine, God sets HIMSELF AGAINST YOU!

I don't want to be there. I want to be found on the grace side. God gives grace to the humble. That's where I want to be found.

I want to seek out those who are qualified to lead, not in the status of their marriage or the discipline of their children but in the humility of their heart. That's the qualification we seek.

I want to live in a church that doesn't split or fight because of doctrinal differences or traditional interpretations. I want to live in a church that offers grace to one another through submission and humility. That works together to be the Body of Christ reaching a lost and dying world.

I want to be part of a church that is committed to grow in faith, bring hope to a dying world, and be known by our love.

And I think you do, too.

Discussion Questions

1. Did you grow up in a church with elders? What was your impression of them?
2. Why do you think it is hard for those of us raised in a democratic society to not see elder selection as a political process?
3. Which of the three Greek terms for elders speaks to you the most? (*elders, shepherd, overseers*) Why?
4. How can you see humility and mutual submission changing the divisions we experience within the church today?

CHAPTER TEN

Alien Burdens

"Two possibilities exist. Either we are alone in the Universe or we are not. Both are equally terrifying."
— Arthur C. Clarke

The old story goes that there was once a man seeking guidance from the Bible. He opened it at random and read, "Judas went out and hanged himself." Flipping quickly to another page, he read, "Go and do thou likewise." In desperation he turned to another page, only to read, "That thou doest, do quickly."

That funny little story illustrates what happens when we take the Bible out of context. Yet it is something we continue to do all the time. We need to understand that when we read the Bible, it isn't a case of us examining it. Rather, it is really the Bible that is examining our lives. The Bible is God's Word — it speaks to us. How we hear that speaking can make a huge difference in our lives!

Obviously, if there is a command that applies to us, we should obey it. If there is a promise, we should take it to heart. If there is a rebuke, we should take heed. We should follow the good examples we see in Scripture.

However, we must be aware of the danger of ripping sentences out of their context. Does 1 Corinthians 3.16 ("You are God's temple . . . God's Spirit dwells in you") teach that Christians should not smoke? No. This verse refers to the church at Corinth rather than to individual Christians. The context is the seriousness of dividing the church. A preacher wanting to teach against smoking would be on safer ground quoting the similar verse in 1 Corinthians 6:19 in which the context is clearly that of the believer's body.

We could list dozens of examples. Why do we take things out of context? Why do we tend to do this with God's Word?

A lot of times, we just aren't as careful with God's Word as we should be. We tend to piece things together through cutting and pasting ideas. Instead of a story of God, we make the Bible into a scrapbook of random quotes. In some ways, it's because of the "verse system" that makes up the layout of our Western Bibles. Because each line is numbered, we tend to separate lines from one another and from the meaning of the whole, so we pull out a verse because it speaks to us. We like the sound of a verse, so we pull it out and repurpose it to say what we want it to say.

Another reason is that we open the Bible with our own preconceived notions. We have our beliefs and our opinions, and we "proof text" our way into making the Scripture say what we want it to say. Instead of opening our mind and heart to allow God to speak to us, we speak to God by twisting the Word to fit our own paradigm. This comes back to the pride that we were discussing earlier. We know what the right things should be, so we use the Bible as a tool (or sometimes even a weapon) to make it mean what we think it should mean.

As we near the end of our study of 1 Peter, we find one of those passages routinely taken out of context by Christians.

Alien Burdens

If you have been a Christian for any length of time, you are probably well aware of 1 Peter 5:7, "casting all your anxieties (care) on him, because he cares for you" (ESV).

In fact, many Christians know this verse by heart, have claimed it in their lives, and even shared it with others in stressful situations. It is a wonderful verse, but unfortunately, we too often apply this verse apart from its context, and in particular, apart from verse 6 to which it is linked and dependent:

> Humble yourselves, therefore, under the mighty hand of God, so that at the proper time he may exalt you. Cast all your anxieties on him, because he cares for you. (1 Peter 5:6-7).

As an introduction and foundation for thinking through 1 Peter 5:6–7, I want to consider a few scriptural propositions with you that I believe are important to our understanding and a proper application of this passage and its counsel concerning our cares.

First, one of the great purposes of God for you and me is that we might be transformed into the image and character of His Son, the Lord Jesus.

This is plainly declared for us in Romans 8:28–29.

"And we know that God causes all things to work together for good to those who love God, to those who are called according to His purpose. For whom He foreknew, He also predestined to become conformed to the image of His Son, so that He might be the firstborn among many brothers and sisters."

Plainly, God wants to make us like His Son.

This transformation is part of the "good and perfect" will of God that He has for each one of us (Romans 12:1–2). Why? it's because this is the place of peace, joy, real meaning in life, and fruitfulness. Only in this way can we be restored to God's purpose for us as human beings.

ALIENATED

Unfortunately, however, we are often more interested in our own will, which is usually wrapped up in our personal wants and plans and in our comfort and pleasure. We want God to care for us, but we want it on our terms and according to our agendas. We ask God to bless our plans rather than seek His direction according to His purposes.

Perhaps nothing manifests the fallen condition of mankind — and this is still true for even regenerated people — like our commitment to operate independently of God. But how do we do this? By trusting in our own resources through which we seek to handle life — find happiness, significance, security, satisfaction, and deal with those problems in life that threaten our agendas or whatever stands in the way of our plans.

The Old Testament prophets often addressed this issue, and to do so, they sometimes used certain word pictures to illustrate this inborn tendency that lies stubbornly in each of us.

The picture of filling your life with the substitutes of the world: In the same way that we might fill an empty bottle, we often seek to fill our emptiness with the world's substitutes to meet life's needs rather than trusting in the Lord and filling our lives with Him and His Word (Isaiah 2:5–12). In Isaiah 2:6, the word *filled* (Hebrew = male) suggests the idea of attempting to remove a void, the problem of personal emptiness, but this is something only God can fill. This word was used in the context of filling something like a pitcher or a bottle with some needed substance (cf. John 7:37–39).

- the picture of lighting our own firebrands by which we seek to direct our way. Rather than trusting God by walking in the light of His Word, we tend to fabricate our own sources of light (Isaiah 50:10–11).
- the picture of sheep that go astray because they are prone to wander and go their own way rather than follow the Lord who is our Shepherd (Isaiah 53:6; Psalms 23).

- the picture of building our own cisterns rather than drinking from God's resources as the one and only Fountain of Living Water; but as it always turns out, our cisterns are broken (Jeremiah 2:12).
- the picture of the arm of the flesh. I am reminded of the picture of the arm and hammer on a baking soda box with the implicit promise that this product will do the job, but the arm of the flesh will not (Jeremiah 17:5). When the term *flesh* is used metaphorically like this in Jeremiah 17:5, what exactly does it mean? It stands for human resources rather than God's resources. Do you see that this idea is present in each of the aforementioned "pictures"?

The "flesh" may be defined as that strong and rebellious nature. Consider the inclination in people to operate out of their own resources to meet their needs and wants, the things they perceive they must have for security and significance. Rather than trust in God, the flesh is a spirit of independence, a commitment to do one's own thing, in one's own way, and from one's own resources. The flesh represents man's attempt to find security, significance, peace, satisfaction, and purpose apart from God, or at least apart from total dependence on Him.

The Bible defines the pursuit of life by our own resources by the word, *pride* or *arrogance*! What is pride? It is man's attempt at becoming his own god, which is pure idolatry. Pride is the position of a swollen estimate of one's own powers, resources, and abilities, causing us, in turn, to ignore God in one way or another.

Several passages of Scripture can be found directly addressing this:

- Deuteronomy 8:11–16 cf. with 8:2–3
- Hosea 13:4–7.

- Habakkuk 2:4–5. The proud live not by faith, but by their own solutions like strong drink to deaden their emptiness or pain. In the process they develop an insatiable appetite for the details of life, which never truly fill their emptiness.
- 1 John 2:16. The Greek word for *life* is *bios*, which refers to what sustains life — the resources needed to live life. The phrase "pride of life" refers to "a boasting or an arrogant independence in one's own resources." It takes an insolent and empty assurance, which trusts in its own power and resources rather than in God and His resources.

Out of God's wisdom, love, mercy, and grace, He wants to draw us to Himself as the only true fountain of living waters, the only source of true refreshment, life, and fruitfulness.

However, because of our propensity to go our own arrogant and independent way, God must operate as a heavenly Father who chastens His sons and as the Vinedresser who cleans and prunes the branches to cause them to abide and keep them healthy and fruitful.

In essence, what is God doing when He prunes or disciplines? He is humbling us. He is working to bring us from the arrogant position of self-dependence, of going our own way and using our own resources to a place of faith/dependence on Him (cf. again Deuteronomy 8:2, 16).

As the Vinedresser, God prunes us to cause us to abide in the Vine, the place of blessing and fruitfulness.

As our loving Father, He disciplines us to bring us to the place of greater and greater faith in Him (Hebrews 12:5, 6, 7 with verses 14, 15a and 3:7f; 5:11f; 10:24–25).

With these propositions in mind, let's look at 1 Peter 5:6–7. Please think of this passage in three movements: (1) The Responsibility or Command: "Humble yourselves under the mighty hand of God."

(2) The Recipe or Procedure: "Cast all your care on Him." (3) The Reason or Motivation: "because He cares for you" (NASB).

The Responsibility

> "Humble yourselves under the mighty hand of God"

The first word, "therefore," directs our attention to the preceding statement of verse 5, "because God is opposed to the proud, but He gives grace to the humble" (NASB).

God is telling us that He is not going to let us get away with arrogant independence without His personal opposition.

But why? Let me suggest two things: First, because the proud person dishonors God. The proud person fails to acknowledge that all that he or she is or has accomplished is ultimately dependent on the Lord.

It's like when a farmer invited a visiting preacher to dinner after the morning service. After a scrumptious meal, most of which was homegrown, the farmer took the preacher out to show him his farm with its rolling landscape complete with fat, well-bred livestock grazing on beautiful green pastures. He saw rows of fruit trees, fields of grain, and a garden that was out of this world. After seeing the beauty of the farm, the preacher commented, "You and the Lord certainly have a beautiful farm here." To this the farmer replied, "Yeah, but you should have seen it when the Lord had it all by Himself."

The proud person will also dishonor and hurt others, even ruining his or her own life. Eventually, pride results in a fall whether it's a person, a church, or nations. This command in 1 Peter 5:6 occurs in a context where leaders are warned against lording it over the flock and where young men are exhorted to submit themselves to elders and all are challenged to clothe themselves with humility. Arrogance is harmful and a hindrance to effective ministry and the body of Christ.

ALIENATED

> Pride goes before destruction, And a haughty spirit before stumbling. It is better to be humble in spirit with the needy, Than to divide the spoils with the proud (Proverbs 16:18–19, NASB).

Mongolian folklore has this wonderful tale of a boasting frog.

Two geese were about to start southward on their annual autumn migration, when they were entreated by a frog to take him with them. The geese expressed their willingness to do so but were at a complete loss as to a means of conveying the frog. The frog ingeniously produced a long, heavy stalk of grass and got each goose to take an end of the stalk while the frog clung to it by his teeth in the middle. In this manner, the three began to make their journey when some men below noticed them. The men loudly expressed their admiration for the device and wondered who had been clever enough to think of it. Whereupon the proud frog opened his mouth to say, "It was I." Needless to say, that was not only the end of the journey for the frog, but also the end of the frog. Pride goes before a fall.

"Humble yourselves" is not perhaps the best translation of the Greek text. Though this is a command and points to a responsibility to obey and respond, the verb in the Greek text is in the passive voice and would be better understood as "be humbled" or "allow yourselves to be humbled." It is somewhat equivalent to "submit yourself to the humbling process of God."

What exactly does it mean to allow yourself to be humbled? Remember that God wants to bring us to the place of humility, which is the place of God- dependence rather than arrogant independence. The reason for this is because dependence on the Lord honors God and is the place of blessing and fruitfulness. It is equivalent to the branch depending on the vine.

One of the key subjects of 1 Peter is suffering. The word *suffer* or the concept of suffering occurs over 15 times in this book. Peter sees suffering (trials) as one of the necessary elements of life.

Alien Burdens

What does suffering do? As a loving Father, God uses suffering or the experience of the tests and trials of life as tools to get our attention and to cause us to grow.

Suffering is designed to turn us from depending on our human strategies to living by faith in Him. It forces our faith to the surface, puts it to work, and purifies it from a life of dependence on ourselves and our solutions like possessing the details of life (cf. 1:6–9, 13–16, 17–21).

Suffering helps us to see our weakness and the insufficiency of our strategies, so we will respond to God's greatness!

On a visit to a museum in Bonn, a young American student became fascinated by the piano on which Beethoven had composed some of his greatest works. She asked the guard if she might play a few bars on it. To help persuade the guard, she also slipped him a lavish tip. The guard agreed and the girl went to the piano and played a short portion of Moonlight Sonata. As she was leaving she said to the guard, "I suppose all the great pianists who come here want to play on that piano." The guard shook his head and said, "Paderewski [the famed Polish pianist] was here a few years ago, and he said he wasn't worthy to touch it."

That young woman wanted the chance to play the piano that Beethoven had played, but what she got was a valuable lesson in humility.

What is humility? Humility is a fitting response to greatness. That applies not only to how people respond to the likes of a Beethoven, but also to how all of us should respond to God.

Now let's turn our attention again to 1 Peter 5:6 and the phrase, "under the mighty hand of God."

Let's note two points about the word *under*.

It draws attention to who we are. We are the creatures and the servants of the sovereign Creator. Regardless of how sovereign men may feel or how much power they may wield, they do not control their own destiny because all are under the sovereign rule of God. In Isaiah 2:22, the Prophet has an interesting and sobering portrait of man's puniness in contrast to God's greatness, which demonstrates how foolish it is for us to put our trust in man, including our own devices by which we seek to find meaning and happiness in life. (2) "Under the mighty hand of God" also stresses who God is. He is the sovereign One, the One who rules over all the universe, which certainly includes our personal world.

- The LORD has established His throne in the heavens; And His sovereignty rules over all (Psalm 103:19).
- But our God is in the heavens; He does whatever He pleases (Psalm 115:3).
- This is what the LORD says: "Heaven is My throne, and the earth is the footstool for My feet" (Isaiah 66:1, NASB).

So where are we? On earth, under God's heaven, living on His footstool and under His authority.

In the phrase, "the mighty hand of God," *mighty* is the Greek word, *krataios*, which refers to strength that is abundantly effective in relation to an end to be gained or dominion to be exercised. Further, in the Old Testament, God's hand symbolized His discipline (Exodus 3:19; 6:1; Psalms 32:4) and His deliverance (Deuteronomy 9:26; Ezekiel 20:34).

These two words reiterate the two points mentioned above:

They remind us of our impotence and insufficiency to handle life on our own.

> I know, Lord, that a man's way is not in himself; Nor is it in a person who walks to direct his steps (Jeremiah 10:23, NASB).

They remind us of God's omnipotence and all sufficiency for whatever life may bring. God's hand is mighty and powerful, and thus able to lead and direct our lives and meet our needs.

This then is a command to submit and allow God to be God and do what He deems necessary regardless of how things may appear to us or how difficult. All things are not good, but because God's hand is mighty and because He is faithful and full of wisdom, He is able to work things together for good, the good of conforming us into the character of Christ.

In the phrase, "that He may exalt you at the proper time," we see the purpose Peter has in mind. The word *exalt* means "to lift up, make high." I am not sure of all that Peter had in mind, but certainly it includes lifting us up from the various places of suffering and persecution, pain and heartache we may face in this life.

Sometimes that lifting up may occur in this life as we experience God's encouragement, deliverance, or success in our work or ministry — but sometimes that lifting up won't happen until the life to come.

No matter how long God delays, we are never to attempt to take matters into our own hands and seek to lift ourselves up by our own human strategies of self-protection. We are to allow God's humbling process to have its transforming effect in making us like His Son.

The lifting up process is first of all a humbling process; the way up is always the way down; the way of death, dying to self-control, is the way of life, the way of becoming a humble servant who gives his life for others as the Savior did for us (1 Peter 2:19–25).

"In the proper time" or in "due time" brings out the element of God's timetable. O, how we need to learn to wait on the Lord. In the pride of leaning on our own strategies, we too often run ahead. We want what we think we need right now, and in our impatience, we turn to our own schemes to get it.

But just how can I manage to do this when everything seems to be going wrong, when Murphy's law seems to be the rule rather than the exception? The recipe, remember, is found in the next verse.

The Recipe

> "casting all your anxiety on him"

"Casting." Note carefully that the text does not command, "cast all your anxiety . . ." This clause is not another command nor the main verb of these two verses, which go together to make up one sentence. True, it has the flavor of an imperative (a command), but in the Greek text, it is not an imperative. Grammatically, this is a verbal participle of means, which tells us how we are to handle the command of verse 6. "Casting" is dependent on the preceding clause and tells us how to "be humbled." We could translate it "by casting all your care on Him."

"Casting" is the Greek verb *epiripto*. It was used of casting garments on a beast of burden. I am reminded of Psalm 68:19, which says, "Blessed be the Lord, who daily bears our burden, The God who is our salvation" (NASB).

The point is, we are to move from the sphere of trusting in our own resources and our strategies for life to resting in God and His resources.

"Anxiety." This is the Greek *merimna*, "care, anxiety, worry." It is used in both a good sense of "godly concerns" and in a bad sense of "worry, anxiety."

It is used of the "worries or cares of the world" that distract men and keep them from spiritual values and priorities that would lead them to faith and a walk with God (Mark 4:19; Luke 8:14; Matt. 13:22; Luke 21:34).

The verb form, *merimnao*, is used in Luke 10:41 of Martha. In contrast to Mary who consistently sat at the feet of Jesus to hear the Word, Martha was consistently distracted with all her preparations (vs. 40) because she was worried and bothered by so many things that, though important, were not the foremost concerns (vs. 41).

It is used in 2 Corinthians 11:28 of Paul's godly concern for the churches.

Here in 1 Peter 5, it is used of any and all our cares whether godly concerns or anxious worry.

"All your anxiety." "All" is the Greek adjective *pas*. When this adjective is in the singular and is used with a singular noun with the article as it is here, it means "the whole" of something. Rather than simply "all your anxiety," the translation, "the whole of your anxiety," drives home the point of the Greek text more forcefully.

The emphasis in this passage is not on casting each individual care, but on casting the whole of one's life on the Lord — lock, stock, and barrel.

It means coming to a place in life where, realizing the Savior's complete sufficiency and our insufficiency (we realize that we can't really handle any part of life apart from the Lord), we then cast the whole of life on Him. By making God's Word a priority, Mary, in contrast to Martha, had done just that (cf. Luke 10:39–42).

We are to give it all to Him not just as our burden bearer, but as our Master, Provider, Trainer, Vinedresser, and heavenly Father. Whether we are facing the irritations of a mosquito or the charge of a lion or elephant, the whole of life is to be cast on Him.

But how can we truly do that? What's the motivation and secret here? This is seen in the final clause of this sentence.

The Reason

> "because he cares for you"

The verb, "cares," is in the present continuous tense, which here undoubtedly looks at a general truth about God. It reminds us that God always and constantly cares about us. It serves to remind us of the unchanging faithfulness and love of God. Life changes and seems terribly fickle, but God's care is steadfast and unfailing, indeed, it is new every morning (Lamentations 3:21–23).

The Greek text is a little more emphatic than the English translation. Literally, the Greek says, "for to Him, it is a care concerning you." This not only says that He cares for us as His children, but that the whole of our care, which He wants us to cast on Him, is very much His personal concern.

According to Bible scholar, Kennth Wuest, the idea is this: "Anxiety is a self-contradiction to true humility. Unbelief is, in a sense, an exalting of self against God in that one is depending upon self and failing to trust God. Why worry therefore, if we are His concern. He is more concerned about our welfare than we could possibly be."[1] Furthermore, He is infinitely more capable of caring for us than we are for ourselves.

In Matthew 6:25–34, the Lord Jesus used basically the same argument to counter anxiety and wrong priorities because of our proneness to anxiety and self-trust. There He reminds us that if God so looks after the birds of the air and the lilies of the field, how much more will He not care for us as our heavenly Father. The issue then is to put first things first, to seek God's kingdom and His righteousness, to rest in His loving care, and to not worry about tomorrow. Tomorrow is in God's hands.

As we cast the whole of our care on the Lord, the need is not only to know that God cares for each of us, but to know that in His care, He is seeking to conform us into the image and character of the Savior (James 1:2–4). For that to occur, it is necessary (1 Peter 1:6) for Him to humble us to move us from the place of self-trust or trust in our own resources into greater and greater levels of faith because God's plan is that "the just shall live by faith."

Though the Bible reveals many reasons for suffering and the trials of life, still, in almost all of them, God is seeking to show us areas where we need to trust Him more; areas where we are in reality living by faith in our circumstances and in our own schemes for handling life.

It just may be, if we are going through some deep waters right now, that God is seeking to reveal areas where we have been leaning on our own resources or trying to run our own life. It may be that we are trying to find our primary satisfaction in something other than the Lord. The fact is real satisfaction apart from the Lord as the source of that satisfaction is a mirage or at best, a vapor that is experienced one moment, and gone the next.

God's counsel concerning our cares is that He cares. "He who did not spare His own Son but gave him up for us all, how will he not also with him graciously give us all things?" (Romans 8:32). We are therefore to cast the whole of our care on Him — not just some areas while we seek to run the others ourselves. The fundamental issue is the need for us to humble ourselves, or to allow ourselves to be humbled and thus also transformed, changed by His sovereign work into the character of His Son. God seeks to move us into greater levels of dependence on Him and out of self-dependent living wherein we seek our joy and happiness or our security, significance, and satisfaction from the details of life rather than from Him. Note the three key elements of the following Psalm — commit (to cast), trust (a walk by faith), and spiritual transformation. We are quick to claim verse 5 and too quick to respond to verse 6.

> Psalm 37:5-6 Commit your way to the Lord, Trust also in Him, and He will do it. And He will bring forth your righteousness as the light, And your judgment as the noonday (NASB).

So give all your worries to God because He is worried about you.

Discussion Questions

1. Think of examples of ways you have seen Scripture taken out of context. Why should we be careful to avoid this?
2. What are some of the "substitutes" with which we fill our lives?
2. What exactly does it mean to allow yourself to be humbled?
3. How does knowing God cares for you change the way you face anxiety? Disappointment?

CHAPTER ELEVEN

Lions, Suffering and Glory (Oh My)

"If aliens visit us, the outcome would be much as when Columbus landed in America, which didn't turn out well for the Native Americans."
— **Stephen Hawking**

"Simon, Simon, Satan has asked to sift all of you as wheat. But I have prayed for you, Simon, that your faith may not fail. And when you have turned back, strengthen your brothers" (Luke 22:31–32, NIV).

Remember the story of Peter's denial? I guarantee Peter does. Satan asked permission from God to have a go at him (ie. Job).

Then Satan answered the Lord, "Does Job fear God for no reason? Have you not put a hedge around him and his house and all that he has, on every side? You have blessed the work of his hands, and his possessions have increased in the land. But stretch out your hand and touch all that he has, and he will curse you to your face." And the Lord said to Satan, "Behold, all that he has is in your hand. Only against him do not stretch out your hand" (Job 1:9–12).

Now, how does Jesus combat that?

Prayer and faith.

Two essential weapons.

We can imagine a picture like this: Satan has a big sieve with jagged-edged wires forming a mesh with holes shaped like faithless men and women. What he aims to do is throw people into this sieve and shake them around over these jagged edges until they are so torn and weak and desperate that they let go of their faith and fall through the sieve as faithless people, right into Satan's company.

Faith cannot fall through the mesh. It's the wrong shape. As long as the disciples hold to their faith, trusting the power and goodness of God for their hope, then they will not fall through the mesh into Satan's hands.

Therefore the sifting of Simon Peter and the others is Satan's effort to destroy their faith. This remains Satan's main goal today. It is relatively unimportant to Satan whether we are healthy or sick, rich or poor; what he wants is to sift out our faith. If he can do it by suffering, he will try that; if he can do it by wealth, he will try that. Peter learned a good lesson that night.

The only person that can fit through Satan's sieve is an unbeliever. The only thing that will fit down the lion's throat is an unbeliever. This is the victory that overcomes Satan's sieve and Satan's throat, our faith (1 John 5:4). If we hold it fast to the end, Satan cannot destroy us. That's why John writes to the church of Smyrna in Revelation 2:10:

> "Do not fear what you are about to suffer. Behold, the devil is about to throw some of you into prison, that you may be tested, and for ten days you will have tribulation. Be faithful unto death, and I will give you the crown of life."

It is encouraging to know that God is infinitely stronger than Satan, and that if we simply trust God to the end, He will give us eternal life. But it is doubly encouraging and doubly hopeful that Jesus Christ and God the Father do not stand back and watch to see if we will have the strength to endure in faith.

In fact, I am sure that if the Holy Trinity were not busy day and night strengthening my faith, it would evaporate in a minute. Notice Jesus prays to his Father for Simon (the word *you* is singular in verse 32: I prayed for "you," that is, Simon). He asks God to do what needs to be done to preserve Simon from destruction.

Jesus is completely confident that his Father will answer His prayer, because He says, "And when you have turned, strengthen your brothers." Jesus knows that Simon will deny him three times. He says so in verse 34. But evidently Jesus does not consider this brief denial to be the utter failure that Satan is after. It is a temporary weakness, a brief faltering of confidence, but it is followed quickly by bitter tears of repentance (Luke 22:62) and turning. Jesus knew he would turn from his sin because He had prayed for him, that his faith not fail utterly.

The Father granted Satan the power to sift Simon, but, in response to Jesus' prayer, he did not let Simon fall through the sieve. Nor will he ever let any of His children fall through Satan's sieve. Here is the double weapon of hope and encouragement that He gives us: Not only is God willing and supremely able to save forever all of us who trust Him, He also conspires with the Son to keep us trusting to the end. We are not left without a shield against the enemy, nor are we left to hold this shield of faith merely by our own strength. God will always see to it that faith has the victory and that His children have faith.

This is the meaning of that terrific text in 1 Peter 1:3–5,

> We have been born anew unto a living hope through the resurrection of Jesus Christ from the dead, and to an inheritance which is imperishable, undefiled and unfading, kept in heaven for you, who by God's power are guarded through faith for a salvation ready to be revealed in the last time.

ALIENATED

Faith, suffering, and glory are all interconnected. Now, return to our current text.

> Be of sober spirit, be on the alert. Your adversary, the devil, prowls around like a roaring lion, seeking someone to devour. So resist him, firm in your faith, knowing that the same experiences of suffering are being accomplished by your brothers and sisters who are in the world. And after you have suffered for a little while, the God of all grace, who called you to His eternal glory in Christ, will Himself perfect, confirm, strengthen and establish you.
>
> To Him be dominion forever and ever. Amen.
>
> Through Silvanus, our faithful brother (for so I regard him), I have written to you briefly, exhorting and testifying that this is the true grace of God. Stand firm in it! She who is in Babylon, chosen together with you, sends you greetings, and so does my son, Mark. Greet one another with a kiss of love. Peace be to you all who are in Christ (1 Peter 5:8-14, NASB).

Peter's first epistle has been dominated by the topic of suffering. In these final verses, for the first time he mentions Satan. Before trying to understand Peter's words here, let us briefly Satan's relationship to suffering review from the Scriptures.

Satan's view of suffering is dictated by his view of success. Because he is success oriented, Satan revels in what he perceives to be success. His head swims with thoughts of his own splendor and glory. His addiction to success led to his own downfall because of his pride and grasping for the preeminence and glory, which belong only to God (see Isaiah 14:12–14; Ezekiel 28:11–15; 1 Timothy 3:6).

Satan also tempts men on the basis of their success. When they are successful, Satan seeks to puff up their pride, convincing them they do not need God (see 1 Chronicles 21:1; 1 Timothy 3:6). But for those who suffer, Satan tries to convince them God cannot be with them, that He cannot care for them because godly people should not suffer.

Let us use the term *glory* rather than today's popular term of *success*. Peter indicates that the themes of suffering and glory both converged in the person of Messiah. But the Old Testament prophets could not understand how this could be since suffering and glory seemed incompatible (see 1 Peter 1:10–12). Satan craves glory, and he employs suffering to turn men from worshipping God to serving him (all the more glory).

Satan's theology of suffering and glory is evident in the temptation of our Lord in the fourth chapters of Matthew (4:1–11) and Luke (4:1–13).

Following the account of Matthew, consider how Satan relates suffering and glory in the temptation of our Lord.

THE FIRST TEMPTATION: MATTHEW 4:1–4

> Then Jesus was led up by the Spirit into the wilderness to be tempted by the devil. And after He had fasted forty days and forty nights, He then became hungry. And the tempter came and said to Him, "If You are the Son of God, command that these stones become bread." But He answered and said, "It is written, 'Man shall not live on bread alone, but on every word that comes out of the Mouth of God'" (Matthew 4:1-4, NASB).

Satan granted Jesus the premise that He was the Son of God, but if He were the Son of God, why was He enduring the suffering of this forty day fast in the wilderness? Jesus should use His power as the Son of God to end His suffering and reveal His glory by commanding that stones become bread.

Suffering was not appropriate for the Son of God, Satan reasoned, but glory could be gained by performing a miracle.

ALIENATED

Jesus' response comes from Deuteronomy 8. There, God indicated through Moses that He purposely led Israel into the wilderness and let them hunger and thirst, so they would learn that men live by God's Word and their obedience to it, not just by eating physical bread. Even if He were to die in the wilderness, He would "live" because life comes from obedience to God's will and to His Word.

THE SECOND TEMPTATION: Matthew 4:5–8

> Then the devil took Him up into the holy city, set Him on the pinnacle of the temple, and said to Him, "If You are the Son of God throw Yourself down; for it is written, 'He shall give his angels charge over you'; and 'in [their] hands they shall bear you up, lest you dash your foot against a stone.'" Jesus said to him, "it is written again, 'you shall not tempt the Lord your god" (Matthew 4:5–7, NKJV).

Satan seeks to intensify the temptation of our Lord by challenging Him to wrongly apply a biblical (and Messianic) promise of protection. God has promised that His angels will protect His "sons" (and especially His Son) from harm. If this promise is true, and if Jesus is truly Messiah, then let Him put God to the test. Let Jesus cast Himself down from the pinnacle of the temple, and then God must act to save Him. Let Him put Himself in a situation where suffering is inevitable, and then God must save Him.

Jesus knew this promise of protection was first and foremost a protection from divine judgment to be fulfilled because He would suffer the wrath of God in the sinner's place. But once again, He employed the principle drawn from the Book of Deuteronomy. Men are not to put God to the test, forcing Him to come to their rescue or do their bidding. Such an action would allow man to become the cause of God's actions, rather than God being the cause of our actions. It is illicit to put God to the test by precipitating suffering.

THE THIRD TEMPTATION: Matthew 4:8–11

Again, the devil took him to a very high mountain and showed him all the kingdoms of the world and their splendor; and he said to Him, "All this I will give you," he said, if you will bow down and worship me." Jesus said to him, "Away from me, Satan! For it is written, 'worship the Lord your God, and serve him only.'" Then the devil left Him, and angels came and attended him (Matthew 4:8–11, NIV).

The first two temptations were primarily about suffering; the third is about glory. Satan shows our Lord the kingdoms of the world and their glory, arrogantly claiming possession of them, a vast overstatement of the truth. He offers these to our Lord if He will but bow down and worship him.

What cheap glory! Cheap in the sense that it was neither Satan's to give nor would it last long. The price was exceedingly high — worship Satan. Satan thought Jesus would be repulsed by suffering and attracted by glory, so he offered Him the glory of earthly kingdoms for the glory Satan would gain by obtaining the worship of Messiah. Oh, to have the Son of God bow down to him!

With no hesitation, Jesus made the reason for His refusal crystal clear: "God alone deserves to be glorified by worship." Jesus knew obedience to God brings glory to Him and leads us to share in His eternal glory. Satan must not be submitted to in worship, for what we worship, we serve. Jesus will not be tempted by cheap glory. His glory will come not in serving Satan but through suffering in the will of the Father.

I believe these same tests were failed by God's "son," Israel (Hosea 11:1; see Matthew 2:15), making the victory of our Lord over these temptations all the more significant. The first test was Jesus' refusal to turn stones into bread. When in the wilderness, God allowed the Israelites to hunger and thirst, so they would learn that obedience to God is the key to life — not just the eating of physical bread (see Deuteronomy 8:1–3). Over and over, the Israelites grumbled against God and threatened to rebel and return to Egypt because they lacked food or water (see Exodus 16; Numbers 11, 14).

During the life and ministry of our Lord, Jesus fed the 5,000. The people followed after Jesus hoping for an eternity of free bread (see John 6:25–34). When Jesus spoke to them about suffering (namely His suffering and their identification with Him), they wanted out. At that point, the crowds left Jesus, and only His disciples remained (John 6:52–69). They wanted the glory of the kingdom, but no suffering. They expected God to turn the stones of suffering into the bread of glory. And this He would do, but only by means of Christ's suffering and their identification with Him in His suffering. This is what baptism was all about.

Our Lord's second test was to cast Himself down so that God would fulfill His promise to protect Him from suffering and harm. The Israelites presumed they could live as they chose, flagrantly disobeying His Word and even rejecting His Son, assuming their privileged position as God's chosen people would force God to save them in spite of their sin. John the Baptist rebuked them for this error, indicating the Son of Man had not come to bless them but to bring judgment upon those who rejected God's Word (see Matthew 3:1–12).

The third test was Satan's proposition that Jesus fall down and worship him, so all the world's glory could be his. Throughout its history, until the Babylonian captivity, the Israelites were idolaters. They worshipped the "gods" whom they trusted to indulge their every fleshly desire. When Moses was absent for a time on the holy mountain, the Israelites had Aaron make them a "god," whom they worshipped by indulging in fleshly and sinful pleasures (Exodus 32:6). The Israelites of Jesus' day chose to reject Him as Messiah to protect and preserve their little kingdom on earth and the glory it provided them, all of which Jesus threatened (John 11:47–50).

Lions, Suffering and Glory (Oh My)

Just prior to Jesus' transfiguration before His disciples, which revealed the glory of His coming kingdom, Jesus began to speak of His suffering and death — a prerequisite to this glory. Peter reacted and rebuked Jesus, seeking to turn Him from suffering to glory. In so doing, Peter was simply reiterating the same temptation Satan put to the Savior in Matthew 4. No wonder Jesus rebuked Peter as Satan. When Satan left Jesus until an "opportune time" (Luke 4:13, NIV), he found that time when Peter sought to rebuke Christ.

Satan's attacks come not only through unbelievers but even through the saints (such as Job's friends).

In the Book of Revelation, John writes to some of the same churches addressed by Peter — the seven churches of Asia (Revelation 2 and 3). In four out of seven churches (2:9, 13, 24; 3:9), John mentions Satan in the context of opposition and suffering. The rest of Revelation teaches that in the last days of history Satan will intensify his efforts to bring about suffering and persecution for the saints. This suffering will serve as a temptation for them to forsake the faith (which appears to be the temptation for the Hebrews). But it will also test and prove the faith of the saints, distinguishing them from the rest of the world.

Now we can understand Peter's reason for establishing the link between suffering and Satan. Peter's warning about Satan's opposition also becomes clearer. Two times in the Gospels, Peter falls prey to Satan's attacks.

The first we see in Matthew 16, where Peter virtually mouths once again the words of Satan recorded in Matthew 4. Speaking for Satan (almost speaking as Satan), Peter rebuked our Lord for bringing up the subject of His suffering because Peter had only thoughts of glory.

In the passage we looked at earlier, Jesus had just given them the promise of glory.

> "You are those who have stood by me in my trials. And I confer on you a kingdom, just as my Father conferred one on me, so that you may eat and drink at my table in my kingdom and sit on thrones, judging the twelve tribes of Israel" (Luke 22:28-30, NIV).

He warned Peter of Satan's demand to "sift him like wheat" (Luke 22:31–32). In those final hours at the Garden of Gethsemene, Peter was not sober, and he did not keep alert to Satan's attacks, so he fell — but not for long.

In reality, Peter's words to us here are his obedience to our Lord's instructions to him in Luke 22:

> "Simon, Simon, behold, Satan has demanded [permission] to sift you men like wheat; but I have prayed for you, that your faith may not fail; and you, when you have turned back, strengthen your brothers" (Luke 22:31-32, NASB, emphasis mine).

We should pay utmost attention to Peter, for he knows only too well whereof he speaks.

I love Peter's imagery of a "roaring lion." It made me ask the question, "Why do lions roar?"

Lions roar to communicate, most often with one another. Lions' roars are a lot like barking dogs. It's about establishing territory. It's about claiming their hunting grounds.

A lion's roar can be heard for up to five miles. It's staking a claim that anyone within the sound of my voice should know that this area is mine.

There is, however, another reason that I find even more applicable to Peter's illustration.

Lions roar right before attacking to instill fear into their prey.

A lion will stalk until he is as close as he can be to the prey. Then he will spring with a roar. The roar disorients and scares the prey into making stupid decisions. Think of deer in headlights. They will freeze,

Lions, Suffering and Glory (Oh My)

they will break off from the herd in a flurry of self-preservation, they will leave the weak and wounded in the herd mentality of fleeing from the danger. All of which serves the lions' purposes.

So how does that apply to Satan stalking churches today?

Suffering and the roar of Satan causes churches and Christians to make stupid decisions. Think of deer in headlights.

They freeze.

Remember, we saw in Jesus' response to Peter the two primary weapons available against the sifting of Satan: prayer and faith. Many will face suffering by freezing and abandoning one or both of those weapons. Their prayer life will falter.

I recently went to the Department of Family and Protective Services (CPS) to minister to those who face evil every day. As I sat with the director, she started crying. She told me the story of her granddaughter. When I asked to pray, she said, "I gotta tell you, my faith is pretty non-existent right now. I can't remember the last time I prayed."

Freezing.

Or they break off from the herd.

A lion will attack the nearest prey. It doesn't test them like wolves or other predators. He takes the most readily available option. So, when he roars, some animals will dart off thinking only of themselves, not realizing that there is more safety within the herd.

People do the same thing. How many people do you know, who when they experience suffering, remove themselves from the church? They feel as if they are supposed to be perfect, so they hide themselves or their problems from those around them.

Breaking off from the herd is one of the worst things you can do Because it leaves the weak and wounded unprotected.

My father-in-law has been known to say, "The army of the Lord is the only force that shoots its own wounded."

Cynical? Yes. Is there is some truth to it? Absolutely. We don't always welcome brokenness, weakness, or wounding within our fellowships. There is an unspoken rule in a lot of churches that you have to fake it till you make it. Pretend we have it all together. Pretend everything is perfect. That is an effect of the roar.

The Scriptures speak of roaring lions, and I believe we should take Peter's meaning from these references:

> "The young lions roar after their prey, And seek their food from God" (Psalms 104:21, NKJV).

- "Is Israel a slave? Or is he a homeborn servant? Why has he become a prey? The young lions have roared at him, they have roared loudly. And they have made his land a waste; His cities have been destroyed, without inhabitant" (Jeremiah 2:14–15, NASB1995; see also 51:36–39).
- "There is a conspiracy of her prophets in her midst, like a roaring lion tearing the prey. They have devoured lives; they have taken treasure and precious things; they have made many widows in the midst of her" (Ezekiel 22:25, NASB1995).

> "Does a lion roar in the forest when he has no prey? Does a young lion growl from his den unless he has captured [something]?" (Amos 3:4).

From these references, it seems clear the explanations above do not fit the picture portrayed in Scripture. The young (not old) lions roar as they pursue their prey and after they have captured it. In this mode of attack, the lion wants his prey to know he is in pursuit. Fear is a part of his plan of attack. A frightened prey is a more likely catch. After the prey is caught, it is devoured, while the lion roars to let all the other creatures know of his victory. The boldness

Lions, Suffering and Glory (Oh My)

and confidence of the lion is likened to the aggressive confidence of Satan, who vainly believes he is invincible.

Peter gives us two commands regarding Satan's attacks. First, we are to be "sober;" second, we are to be "alert." Twice already, Peter has instructed us to be sober (1:13; 4:7). Jesus often exhorted His disciples to be "alert" (Matthew 24:42; 26:41; Romans 13:11f.; 2 Timothy 4:5). In 1 Thessalonians, both terms occur together:

> "So then let us not sleep as others do, but let us be alert and sober. For those who sleep do their sleeping at night, and those who get drunk get drunk at night. But since we are of [the] day, let us be sober, having put on the breastplate of faith and love, and as a helmet, the hope of salvation" (1 Thessalonians 5:6-8, NASB1995, emphasis mine).

Most often these terms are employed in the context of the last days. The disciples must not be caught off guard; they are to be mentally alert, so the events preceding our Lord's coming do not cause them to panic, for many, in Peter's words, will be devoured (see Matthew 24:3–14, 32–44).

As I understand our Lord's teaching concerning the last days in the Gospels (Matthew 24 and 25; Mark 13; Luke 12; 21; John 13–16), in Paul's epistles (e.g. 1 Thessalonians 5:1–11; 2 Thessalonians 2:1–12) and in the Book of Revelation, they will be marked by increased opposition and persecution toward the saints. Satanic activity and opposition will also increase. The saints are therefore exhorted to be alert and sober, so these difficult days do not throw them off balance.

I believe Peter's words in our text imply a shortness of time and an increase in persecution. He wants us to recognize that Satan will seek to destroy us through the opposition of unbelievers. He wants us to be ready for what is coming and not be surprised when it comes upon us. Recognizing Satan's hand in the difficulties we face, we must resist him.

ALIENATED

The key to Peter's survival under Satan's attack was his faith, just as our Lord had prayed for him that his faith would not fail. Faith is, likewise, the key to our resisting Satan's attacks.

But why faith? Why is faith so essential? Because Satan's attacks against the believer are an attack on faith itself. When Satan tempted Adam and Eve, he tried to induce them to act independently (disobediently) of God. They were urged to act independently of God by Satan, raising doubts in their hearts about the trustworthiness of God. They could not understand why God would "hold back" the fruit of the forbidden tree and what it offered. They trusted in themselves (and Satan) by doubting God. When we are successful, Satan tempts us with pride, seeking to turn us from God because we think we no longer need Him. When we suffer, Satan tempts us with doubt and unbelief, trying to make us believe God has abandoned us, so we will act independently of God to bring about what is in our best interest — or so we think.

Peter's comments in verses 9 and 10 provide us with much fuel for faith. First, we can be firm in our faith because we know we are not alone in our suffering. Furthermore, we are well aware that many others who are suffering for their faith are standing fast as well. When we suffer, we are tempted to think our situation is unique, that no one has ever faced the difficulties we are facing. Thus, the standard biblical solutions and principles cannot apply to us; we are exceptions to the rule. This mindset is in direct contradiction to the Word of God, for we read,

> [13] No temptation has overtaken you but such as is common to man; and God is faithful, who will not allow you to be tempted beyond what you are able, but with the temptation will provide the way of escape also, that you may be able to endure it (1 Corinthians 10:13, NASB1995).

Lions, Suffering and Glory (Oh My)

The second basis for a firm faith is knowing that even though Satan seeks to destroy us, God sovereignly uses his opposition to further His purposes and strengthen our faith. As Peter has already shown, trials and suffering are the means by which our faith is proven (1 Peter 1:7). Now, he will say so again. Suffering is the means by which God — the God of all grace — perfects, confirms, strengthens, and establishes us (1 Peter 5:10). The very trials that may appear to be the means Satan employs for our destruction are the means God employs for our deliverance and development. Behind the opposition of unbelievers stands Satan seeking to devour us, and behind Satan stands God, sure to perfect and purify us.

The third basis for our faith is found in 1 Peter 5:11: "To Him be dominion forever and ever. Amen" (NASB1995).

Satan claims to control much more than he does (see Matthew 4:9) and even demands that which is not his (Luke 22:31). He seeks dominion over all the earth and over the people of God, but dominion does not belong to him; it belongs to the Lord Jesus, whose death, burial, and resurrection brought about Satan's downfall (John 16:11; Ephesians 1:18–23; Colossians 8:15; 1 Peter 3:21–22).

Finally, Peter exhorts the suffering saints to whom he writes to "greet one another with the kiss of love" (verse 14, ESV). This command is found several times in the New Testament (Romans 16:16; 1 Corinthians 16:20; 2 Corinthians 13:12; 1 Thessalonians 5:26). Here is a command few, if any, Christians take seriously today. Since the command is repeated five times in the New Testament, we may need to reconsider it.

The commanded kiss is a holy kiss, not a Hollywood kiss. It is a token or expression of our love for one another. As I understand the "kiss" in that time and culture, it probably was not men kissing women, but men kissing men and women kissing women. No sexual connotation was involved. The command is therefore to give a visible, symbolic expression of our love for one another. Our love for one another is the essence; our greeting one another with a kiss is the secondary expression.

The most important thing to remember is not to allow opposition from the outside to hinder or diminish our love for one another.

Though we may not physically kiss one another, we do share fellowship together. This fellowship is much more than merely "going to church." This is shoring up our own faith as well as providing faith for those who are being sifted.

If you are in that place, if you feel as if you are being "sifted," do not remove yourself. You need the church. You need prayer and faith. Even if you cannot pray yourself, you need faithful brothers and sisters to lift you up. Even if your faith is weak, you need brothers and sisters to believe for you.

Prayer and faith are our response to satanic attacks. You cannot do it alone.

Don't let the roar cause you to fear. Don't let the roar cause you to freeze. Don't let the roar drive you away from the church.

The only way you will face this trial is through prayer and faith.

Discussion Questions

1. How does Jesus combat Satan in regard to his "sifting" of Peter? How then should we use the same weapons in battle against him today?

2. Contrast the satanic view of suffering and success with the Christlike view of suffering and glory. How are they different and how do those differences affect our reactions?

3. Why is faith so essential in resistance of Satan's attacks?

CHAPTER TWELVE

Living in an Alien Nation

"I personally don't believe in aliens. But, I do believe that there is something out there that is accountable for all these mysterious things that are going on: I think it is a spiritual thing, not a material thing."
— J.T. Walsh

The only monument in the world built in the shape of a bug, to honor a bug is located in Enterprise, Alabama. In 1915 the Mexican boll weevil invaded Southeast Alabama and destroyed 60 percent of the cotton crop. In desperation, the farmers turned to planting peanuts. By 1917 the peanut industry had become so profitable that the county harvested more peanuts than any other county in the nation. In gratitude, the people of the town erected a statue and inscribed these words,

"In profound appreciation of the Boll Weevil and what it has done as the Herald of Prosperity." The instrument of their suffering had become the means of their blessing."

Sometimes, thankfulness and gratitude are all about perspective. Think back over the course of your life. Like me, you can probably think of many things you believed were "instruments of suffering" that turned out to be "means of blessing."

This week, you may feel like you're in the middle of a storm. You may feel abandoned and neglected and wonder if God even cares about you. But remember the boll weevil in Southeast Alabama. Also remember that throughout Scripture, God routinely begins His greatest works when people are in the wilderness.

Whether it was the children of Israel entering the promised land, David becoming king of Israel, or Jesus beginning His earthly ministry; all of these began with time in the wilderness.

The trending wisdom in churches today seems to be something like this: "God just wants me to be happy. God just wants me to be fulfilled. God just wants me to be prosperous and successful. As long as I give Him the glory, God just wants me to have whatever I want."

I once was told that I needed to "speak victory" over a problem. I was told that if I simply claimed victory in the name of Jesus, that it would be so. Then I found this in my Facebook feed from a friend of mine.

If you want success, if you want wisdom, if you want to be prosperous and healthy, . . . you must boldly declare words of faith and victory over yourself and your family.

Then I saw a video of a pastor of a church in Dallas, and he said, "The church is growing because we are teaching people that God just wants you to be happy. We are showing them that poverty is from the devil and that God wants all Christians prosperous"

Everywhere I look, that seems to be the message of Christianity today. And that message works. People flock to it in droves. The idea that God just wants you to be happy is intoxicating. It calls people to it. It draws people in. It makes people giddy with excitement over all the bounty that is just waiting to be lavished upon them.

But there's a huge problem with this whole idea: It isn't true.

It isn't true, biblical, or what the prophets taught. It isn't what Jesus taught, and it isn't what His apostles taught.

As we have walked through Peter's letter to these churches, we have encountered people who would soon endure serious and severe persecution. What we haven't seen is any of the "name it and claim it" prosperity gospel that pervades American Christianity. Instead, we might argue that we see the opposite. The idea in 1 Peter seems to be that God wants you in the wilderness.

That idea doesn't sell as well. The wilderness is wild and desolate. There is no victory in the wilderness — only survival. There is no power and prestige in the wilderness. There is no celebrity or bounty found in the wilderness. Yet, I'm convinced that that is where God finds me the best.

There are lots of wildernesses.

- Spiritual wilderness, when you feel removed and disconnected from God.
- Emotional wilderness, when you feel separated from everyone.
- There are wildernesses into which we have accidentally wandered.
- There are wildernesses where we arrived by choices we have made.

Regardless of what your wilderness is or what caused you to be there, finding God in the wilderness is a key to living the abundant life Jesus came for us to share.

Take David for example.

After David killed Goliath, his celebrity dominated Israel. People wrote songs about him. Saul made him a leader of men and sent him out in hopes that he would be killed, but that only served to further his fame. He was the king's son-in-law. He's the champion of Israel. He was a star.

Wouldn't the next step be to become king? It had been promised to him. It seemed logical to Saul that the next step would be to make David king.

But that wasn't the step God chose.

After the third time Saul tried to pin him to the wall with a spear, David had gotten the message. He realized that wasn't a problem he could kill. He had to run. So, he ran and as he did, we see all his crutches, all his supports, all his security blankets stripped away from him one by one.

David was systematically stripped of everyone and everything on which he depended. Driven into the wilderness, David finally stopped in a cave and wrote the words of Psalm 142:

> "there is none who takes notice of me; no refuge remains to me;
> no one cares for my soul" (Psalm 142:4).

Keep in mind here, David had done nothing wrong. He had not disobeyed. In fact, he had been the model of humility, dependability, and integrity. Yet God began to systematically remove every crutch, every security blanket from David's life.

For a young man, this must have been a faith-shaking experience. Here he was, the anointed of God, the chosen one, following the will of God to the best of his ability . . . when the bottom started falling out.

First, he lost his position. David had been promoted to the captain of the King's army. He led all the men into battle. He was a celebrity. People loved him. They sang songs about him and danced in the streets as he returned from his latest exploit. Yet that very celebrity lit the fire of a jealous rage inside Saul. David had no choice but to become a fugitive, an outlaw, hunted by the same army he had once led.

Then he lost his wife. Although Michal loved David, Saul tried to use her to get to him. He sent men to grab David at home, when his guard would be down. Michal smuggled him out a window and covered for him until he could escape. Then, trapped between her husband and her father, she lied. "I had to help him!" she told her father, "He threatened to kill me if I didn't" (19:17). And David lost his wife.

They would be brought together again years later, but never again would Michal's heart be joined with David in the same way. So, David lost his wife.

Next, he lost his mentor. David fled to Samuel, the one who had anointed him, his connection with the voice of God, his mentor. Surely, he would be safe there, for Saul would never lay hands on the prophet of God. Wrong again. Saul pursued him, and once more, David had to flee. David ran for his life, and this was the last time he would ever see his cherished mentor. Even when Samuel died, David wasn't free to attend the funeral. So, another crutch, another security blanket, was removed.

He also lost his friend. When David left Samuel, he fled to his friend, Jonathan. From their first meeting, these two had been joined in soul and spirit. Thzeir friendship was sacred. David would later write, "Jonathan my brother, you were very dear to me. Your love for me was wonderful, more wonderful than that of women" (2 Samuel 1:26, NIV). At first, Jonathan refused to believe his father was so far gone that he would kill David. Finally, when Saul threw a spear at his own son in a fit of rage for helping David, Jonathan had to acknowledge it was too late. And David lost his friend.

David then ran to a place called Nob. In 2 Samuel 21, in his desperation to save himself, he tried to shape God to fit his own needs. He had, throughout all of this, failed to inquire of the Lord. He was only running. Only thinking of survival. And when he got to Nob, he lied to the priests to fulfill his own needs. That lie would come back to haunt him. Because at Nob, David losts his integrity.

ALIENATED

Finally, with nowhere else to turn, David fled to the land of the Philistines. Blindly running. Hoping to get away. Thinking only of himself. Concerned only with survival, he found himself at a place called Gath, which was one of the five chief Philistine city-states. Remember that name? Heard it before? It's because Gath was the home of... Goliath. As David ran, he thought only of escape from Saul. Then he realized where he was. All those "ten thousands" that the people of Israel sing about, those were Philistines. The 100 dead dowry that Saul demanded, which David doubled to 200? Those were Philistines. And as he stood at the city gates, he realized that he had run from one threat into the arms of another, so he pretended to be crazy.

He scratched at the gate. He drooled all over himself. He pretended to be insane. And at Gath, the final blow, David lost his dignity.

David ran to the cave at Adullam. He had lost his position, his wife, his mentor, his friend, his integrity, and his dignity and he was about as low as a man could get. Stripped of all pride. Trapped. At the end of his rope. He ran to Adullam. A notorious hangout of outlaws. A place with an underground labyrinth of caves.

Later, Christians would hide here. Even today, guides fear this place because a man could lose himself in there and never come out.

As David penned the words of Psalm 142, "no cares about me," many of today's teachers would tell him, "David, you just need to claim victory. Speak victory over your life, and it will all change. You just need more faith, David. God wants you to be happy. God wants you to be fulfilled."

When the truth is... David was EXACTLY where God wanted him.

Are you in a cave? Are you at the end of your rope? Have you reached a place where you feel like everything that you cherished has been stripped away from you? Maybe you are right where God wants you.

Peter learned this the hard way. He found himself many times in wildernesses, and each time, he was where God wanted him to be.

When the disciples were in the boat, and it was being buffeted by the waves, it was because Jesus had sent them on ahead. Let that sink in for moment. Jesus sent them into the storm. Into the wilderness. It was there, in that storm, that they would see His glory. It was there that they would experience His power. It was there that they would truly encounter God.

The same thing happened to David.

David came out of the cave. You can, too. Not through some hocus pocus of positive thinking nonsense but through following the same path he took.

First, David looked up.

David found himself by finding God. By reopening dialogue with the Lord. Throughout all this, David had relied on these crutches. He had clung to these security blankets. Yet they could not sustain him.

Many times, our security blankets become substitutes for God. The Bible calls that idolatry. Whether it's our position, our mate, our children, our mentors, our friends, whatever the crutch; when it becomes more important than God, it is an idol.

David finally hurt enough to stop looking at himself. David had finally been brought low enough that he could admit his need. He cried out in the only way he knew how — he cried out to the Lord.

The first turning point for David comes in 1 Samuel 23:2, "Therefore, he inquired of the Lord . . ." (NIV).

The first step out of the cave is to seek God. Call on Him. Cling to Him for refuge and safety. When we stop relying on crutches, when we stop clinging to security blankets, and when we stop trusting in ourselves, we can begin to step out of the cave.

Second, David owned up.

He began to recover his integrity by facing the dirty, ugly truth of some of his actions. When Abiathar went to the cave and recounted

ALIENATED

to David how Saul slaughtered the entire village of Nob — all the priests, every woman, every child, every animal. It hit David.

This is my fault.

Anyone would have known Saul would have made Nob pay for helping David. Yet at that moment, he didn't care that his lies jeopardized the lives of an entire town.

"I have occasioned the death of all the persons of your father's house" (1 Samuel 22:22). *The blood is on my hands. It's my fault. I did this.* David genuinely repented.

We can't fix things by brooding over what we've lost. The best grief is one that leads us out of our own blind self-preoccupation. Accepting responsibility for our deceptions, our callousness, our self-centeredness is a first and indispensable step toward healing.

Repenting and owning our part in our sins is a key step in walking out of the cave.

Third, David stood up.

David regained his dignity when he resumed his God-given leadership and again began acting like the Lord's anointed. The cave psalm (Psalm 42) ends, "Then the righteous will gather about me" (v. 7, NIV).

And they did. They went to the cave at Adullam in droves. Hundreds of them. David's family went. Those who were distressed, indebted, desolated and desperate went to David. The discontented, the disheartened, those who had nowhere else to go — they all went to David.

From this group of rejects, malcontents, and failures, God raised up an army of over 600 men. David would find his "mighty men" here. His inner circle. His elite squad. Men who would perform amazing heroic efforts and be heroes throughout all Israel. They started out in the cave, too.

You see, sometimes the cave is where God wants you to be.

I know it isn't popular. Today, it's popular to hear that following God will fix all your problems. You just name it and claim it, and God will fix it all. But that isn't true.

Sometimes, God is in the business of stripping away all the other things that you are leaning on so that you will lean on Him.

The wilderness is a sacred place. God does miraculous things in the wilderness.

Let me say to you, if you find yourself in the wilderness, be encouraged. All the great works of God begin in the wilderness.

Moses found the burning bush . . . in the wilderness. Before the Israelites could claim the promised land, they spend 40 years . . . in the wilderness. Before David, though anointed, could be crowned king, he had to first find himself . . . in the wilderness. Jesus began His ministry by spending 40 days . . . in the wilderness.

If you are in the wilderness, I submit that you are *exactly* where God wants you to be. He is stripping away all the crutches, all the idols, and all the security blankets so that you can totally trust in Him.

To do that, you must cry out to Him. Look up. Take your focus off all the junk around you and look to heaven. That's your refuge. Your shelter. Your strength.

Then you must repent. You must own up to your part in this journey. You must admit and acknowledge that some of your own choices, your own failures, your own sins got you here. When you can do that, God can change your heart.

And then you stand tall. Stop feeling sorry for yourself. Stop mourning what you've lost. Focus on God, and allow Him to put you in the place where He wants you to be. That may be as a leader. It may be as a servant. It may be simply leading others out of the cave.

The great miraculous works of God begin in the wilderness.

Peter has spent this entire letter preparing and equipping these alienated believers for the wilderness that was about to overtake them. He wanted them to understand their place in God's plan, the use of suffering for the betterment of their faith and to trust in the One who will meet them there in that wilderness.

Hopefully, you have heard that as well. You have heard the voice of God in the wilderness. You have felt the presence of God in the wilderness. You have felt your faith being strengthened as your hope is being built up.

You are alienated. You are in a wilderness of strange things, strange people, and strange struggles. Yet there is One who is greater, who seeks you, who comes to you, and who will lead you home.

Discussion Questions

1. What are some examples of the prosperity gospel that you have seen in Christian culture?

2. Can you think of a time in your life when God met you in the wilderness?

3. What advice would you give to one who is currently in the wilderness?

4. What do you think, based on our study, Peter would say to someone experiencing suffering in the wilderness?

www.ingramcontent.com/pod-product-compliance
Lightning Source LLC
Chambersburg PA
CBHW070157100426
42743CB00013B/2949